CH00871802

EYES OF THE

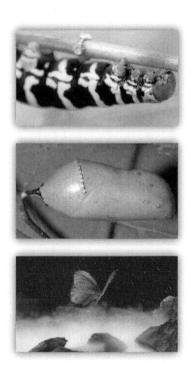

SHOWCASING EXCITING NEW POETS
EDITED BY ANGELA FAIRBRACE

spotlight poets

First published in Great Britain in 2007 by
Spotlight Poets
Remus House
Coltsfoot Drive
Peterborough
PE2 9JX
Telephone: 01733 898101
Fax: 01733 313524
Website: www.forwardpress.co.uk
Email: spotlightpoets@forwardpress.co.uk

SB ISBN 978-1-84077-165-7

Foreword

Spotlight Poets was established in 1997 as an imprint of Forward Press Ltd in a bid to launch the best of our poets into the public sphere. Since then we have worked hard to present our authors' work in a way that not only complements their style but reflects the class of poet they undoubtedly are.

All the authors in our Spotlight Poets series are hand-selected on the basis of creativity, style and flair, not to mention form and appeal. As a nation of poetry lovers, many of us are still reluctant to venture into the realms of 'new' and 'unknown'. For those of us that would like to take an interest in the poetic art form or for those of us already holding it in high esteem it can be nigh on impossible to find quality new authors and material. Well, we present this to you... Spotlight Poets has opened up a doorway to something quite special.

Within, readers can not only revel in the best of our authors but also take a look at the lives of our poets and what inspires them. Each author has the chance to provide a biography and photograph to allow the reader to take a peek at their contemporaries. As contemporaries ourselves, we love the chance to get involved and take a deeper look at a collection of work. We hope you do too.

Angela Fairbrace
Editor

CONTENTS

THE POETS & THEIR
FEATURED COLLECTIONS

DAVID AUSTIN

I started writing back in the late sixties when I penned lyrics for the youth club rock band. It wasn't long before my lyrics developed into more complex patterns of words and became 'poetry'. I started writing in free verse and that remains my favourite form to this day, although my rhyming poems have brought me a lot of acclaim too. My greatest influence and inspiration is derived from my happy childhood and also, conversely, the destructive effects of passing time. I love using alliteration in my work, which I find to be a powerful expressive device, and I have won various awards in poetry competitions. I also write short stories, mostly with supernatural themes, and I have written articles for a large circulation Yorkshire nostalgia magazine. My other main hobby is photography, and I like to photograph nature, especially flowers. I am out with my digital cameras most sunny days in the open spaces in and around Sheffield, where I was born and still live. I love the city and its surrounding countryside, which has provided further inspiration for my work. I am divorced after fifteen years of marriage, and I recently took early retirement through ill health. I now devote most of my time to hobbies. I am not a prolific writer and usually only write for the exigencies of magazines and competitions. My favourite poets are Dylan Thomas and Ted Hughes. I read a lot of novels and biographies. I also read childhood memoirs. My poems are well received by editors and have been published, not only in this country, but also in far flung places such as India. Some of my short stories have also been published by Forward Press in their New Fiction imprint.

Child

When sun's red disc fired cloud-strands of dawn,
And the playground was damp with dew,
I, fresh from dream, stretched young legs,
Raised wondrous eyes to vibrant Heaven
And gulped morning air like my first breath.

It was another beginning: fresh spray
Sprinkled cool flesh, seas thundered on breakers
In the moving sand. O how my body
Worshipped the breeze, and joy filled
A whole dome of sky.

I commanded the sighing foam: it was flux
Between my toes. Tingling feet kicked
A dazzle of droplets in sun-streaked air,
They fell onto wavelets, rained
In my salt-caked hair:
A shower of molten gold.

Then back to the playground: a swing's arc
Carried me through cool blue. It was six years
Since birth, I was a silk-skinned traveller
In a new world: fresh fruit in a strange orchard
Of sensations.

I ran: legs flashing like seagull's wings
In sunlight. I flew over emerald grass, flowers
Shining in a green cosmos. Bare feet
Treading galaxies of daisies. I was a meteor,
Chasing echoes of laughter
Through sparkling dominions.

Incipient power of growing stirred a storm:
Taut energy released, I was catapulted
Through environs of dreams, down a slide of days,
A multitude of dawns.
Fresh and pure, forever plunging
Into foam-curled waves:
Gliding with the high gulls -
And always, always the child.

Moth

Folded wings,
Veined as marble,
Are like a black
Pythagorean triangle:
A ship's sail's
Sunset silhouette
Against the bright glare
Of the lamp.

Aimless circled wanderings
On the shade,
Are perhaps a quest for freedom
From the attraction of light:
Like my quest
To escape temptation,
My blind adventures
In life's ravelled maze.

Take flight, moth,
Beyond the window,
Glee-driven wings
Dusted with hope:
Midnight's unsung freedom
Awaits.

I will follow this example
Of graceful escape,
Will leave the confines
Of my weaknesses.

Dormant adrenaline awakes,
Eager youth,
Victim of gradual
Submission to time -
Returns.

Lost Garden

(For my youngest brother, Robert, who is mentally handicapped and now lives in Local Authority care)

The hay cart rots in clinging grass,
And rain slants through the day.
Old rusting wheels with hubs of brass,
Sink in the sodden clay.

Here fading foxgloves sadly hang
On dehydrated stalks,
And under trees where blackbirds sang,
The ghost of childhood walks.

Now all is quiet, where I wheeled
My hay cart over earth:
In silent supplication, kneeled -
To greet my brother's birth.

I knew not then he'd never shin
High oak trees in the lane,
Or he possessed beneath his skin
An oxygen-starved brain.

Now he resides so far away
And memories are gone,
Of silver skies and hay cart play,
When he was less than one.

He never knew the sway of trees,
Where feathered breezes blow,
Nor felt the numbing winter freeze,
And gentle kiss of snow.

Instead he sat within his room
And spent his early years,
Unheeding an impending gloom,
Concealed in falling tears.

Now in the garden chaos reigns:
Flowers and weeds entwine,
In protest at my brother's pains,
And indirectly mine.

The garden's lost inside my head:
Once close-razed lawns aren't mown,
The velvet foxgloves now are dead,
And all the birds have flown.

DAVID AUSTIN

Eskdale

On choppy seas of low cloud,
Slate-peak islands
Float rain-blotted deeps:
Dark mammoth hill-heads
Obscure cold space,
Their strewn boulders

Jammed in jumbled symmetry:
Dislodged, they would fall
Into alien worlds: deep
Valleys of men and time.

Absolute silence fine tunes
To a perfect pitch of peace
The black bell of night,
Its east rim gilded
By a cloud-feathered sun.

Dawn is an intruder,
Returning bleating life,
To slate-slabbed dominions
Of scattered sheep.

Villanelle For A Dove

Beating wings facile in the frosty air,
As snowy skies from far horizons loom,
A white dove rises from its winter lair.

Purity and beauty beyond compare,
Ghosting the borders of a tree-dark gloom,
Beating wings facile in the frosty air.

Symbol of peace that soothes a dark despair,
Where gnarled, looped branches tremble and entomb,
A white dove rises from its winter lair.

Faint Christmas stars briefly blossom and flare,
Light softly shining in my winter room:
Beating wings facile in the frosty air.

Cold, gauzy cloud dims a swollen moon's stare,
Mirrored in ice like a petrified bloom:
A white dove rises from its winter lair.

Earth in iron grip, the bent trees leaf-bare,
Roots snow-deep, and above their drifted womb -
Beating wings facile in the frosty air;
A white dove rises from its winter lair.

Doll

Abandoned in the swaying grass,
That blows beside a narrow lane,
Where pacing people seldom pass;
She lies exposed to drifting rain.

Forlorn beneath the circling skies,
A hidden hollow hides her form:
Soft raindrops are the tears she cries,
Sprayed from the remnants of a storm.

Where are the loving arms that held
Her flaxen head in fond embrace?
The cherished gaze unparalleled,
Persisting from a faultless face -

The sweet face of a perfect child,
Who sheltered her in clasping hands;
A little girl yet undefiled;
She skipped through softly shifting sands.

The sands of time then slowly yield:
She fell headlong into its whirl:
The fresh growth of a summer field,
Is stunted by the winter's pearl.

Her cheeks now like a wrinkled prune,
And innocence defiled near death,
The child who long since passed her noon,
Is old and worn with laboured breath.

The doll still has a youthful bloom,
Although the child succumbed to time,
And still glows in the grasses' gloom,
In summer warmth and winter rime.

Butterfly

There is no savagery or ruthless vice
In this unchained flower,
Dragon-flamed wings ignited
By the snaking-grasses fuse.

Mantras of war are for birds, beasts and men
To chant incessantly
Until they draw
Their last rattling battle-breath:

You rise from the killing-grounds
To celebrate the sun,
A nectar-primed power-pack
Crackling with the potency of flight:

Flashing over a tree-bordered twilight of water,
Born with the weed-seed
On singing sedge-combed breezes
Which stir the haystack's flaxen thatch:

You are an aeolian ghost:
Brought on a wind of dreams from lost childhood,
Red admiral of blushing skies
Haunting sorrel-smoked spinneys of summer:

Evoking from time-buried years,
A laughing, bright-eyed innocence, which drove
My agile body through swaying wheat-field dawns
Dense with the kindling colours of quivering wings.

I caught you clinging to a bending poppy's plume,
Like a fragment of the setting sun,
Ephemeral as smoke, yet graceful in your dying,
Bowing out to the cloud-crinkled evening.

Time Flies

Driven by the taught spring of youth,
I feel immortal,
Inviting childish laughter
Into my ignorance of old age.

Sapling-supple bones
Arrayed in summer flesh,
Move in a celebration
Of lively warmth.

Unheeded,
A winter hatches in the marrow:
Spreads unhurried disorder
Through green age:

Too soon the joy of my body
Will be ash,
Bricked in a wall of remembrance,
Which will easily be forgotten.

Childhood Home

I stood in a grip of ice
That froze and tossed these old walls
In a tumble of time.
This now-roofless shell,
Which once cradled my
Incipient warmth,
Wrapped my formative years
In a strong embrace
Of sun-stretched days,
And moon-mingled nights
Where quick cats darted through
The garden's sleeping flowers.

Magical summers sang
Their high notes
Through crowded raspberry canes,
And blown poppies blushed
Where dancing emerald blades of grass
Tickled my freshly formed feet
In whispers of fluting air.

Glancing on my early bed,
A lone, bright star
Set in window glass
Shone faintly on my face
As I painted mind-pictures
From wallpaper patterns,
And watched
Faraway house lights
Ripple with curtained thoughts.

Crackling, smoky autumn fires:
Sledges sliding lamp-lit tracks
In the cream of winter snows,
Curl back on a tide of years

To soak the cold, empty shell
In happy life once more:
And this sudden rush of memory
Brings my singing childhood home.

Autumn's Reflection

The cold astronomy of night
Imprints the autumn chill,
And in the gale a crying voice
Tells tales from overseas:
'The soldier's boots are clods of mud'
'And bayonets slash the moon'
'A starving child gropes for a hand

To guide him through the war'
And leaves in England drift like waves
From green and brown to gold,
Reflecting pain that memory hides
Within its prison walls,
And the government will always win
The losses of the world,
As a poor man fights with waning strength
To keep a wife and child.

Too many hearts of stone exist
In the morning of a dream,
And fail to sense outside themselves
The wide expanse of love.
As winter's shadow covers fields
In quiet lands of snow,
The beast of progress devastates
The root of all that's true.

And no one ever will return
To journey paths of sun,
Where a wasteland lies beneath the stars
Over which my words are flung.

Like empty caves in which the lies
Of nations echo through,
The hollow years destroy the smiles
Of those who breathe anew.

ROSEMARY BENZING

Born in Vizagapatam, South India and brought up in Stretford, Manchester. Defining childhood moments include being one of seven hundred children at Stretford Grammar School communally mourning the Munich Air Disaster and being only yards away when Simon Sandys Winsch was killed in the TT races.

Studied English, philosophy and psychology. Trained and worked as teacher, counsellor and occasional freelance journalist. Also worked as auxiliary psychiatric nurse in student holidays.

Married with a grown-up son and daughter. Lives in a rural Shropshire village with husband. Enjoys trips to London for theatre visits, walking along Cornish sea cliffs, gardening. Loves cats, reading and playing the piano. Favourite cities - London, New York, Barcelona. Favourite beauty spots - Bedruthan Steps, the Amalfi Coast, Cephalonia and Deya, Majorca.

My Very Dear

Dorothy, I am glad John has his heart's desire.
He has waited for the girl to inspire
him and you are his first and only love.
We shall give you above all
a welcome into our family.
I wonder when that will be.

Though I suppose I should disguise
my pride, I think you have drawn a prize.
I hope you will both be very happy.
We heard about your father's bravery
on the radio and in the papers.
My own Vivien is in the next Birthday Honours.
He has been awarded a CBE.
My love, dear little daughter
soon to be.

School Passport

Filling in the form Gran lied.
As she put it, 'Information
placed in the wrong hands
leads to trouble.
Let not your friend your secret know.
What's in a birthplace
or an ocean between friends?'

Still Life With Jam Jar

No pets but a lemon curd jar,
some post-war brand
with cardboard lid
punched with pencil holes.
Inside a glut of caterpillars,
apple-green, segmented like the brain
and wiry black and gold.

I fed them on nasturtium
leaves and the occasional seed.
While I waited for them to turn
to cabbage-white and red admiral,
they proved my father right when he said
we should all go pop with a second helping.
I found their flattened husks around the jar.
Prizing off the lid, the innards
of all thirty-eight, ripened avocado.

Once Upon A Time

The day Mother killed the cat
we took in as a stray,
'I don't wish to discuss it further
in my state of health,' was all she'd say.

The day she fetched two policemen
at 2am to take me away,
'I don't wish to discuss it further
in my state of health,' was all she'd say.

The day my dad was killed in the crash,
the pastor said, ' Take off your glasses and pray!'
He didn't have them on that day,
'Let's not discuss it,' was all she'd say.

Under The Weather

Carry me with balsam.
My bean shoots are clogged
and my bloom washed out,
a pasty shadow under the birdsong.
Leaves flutter their flaps,
set the moon under wraps.

Hammock lurches
as wisteria takes over,
curling its tendrils.
While bees suck their fire
a blaze of montbretias
point their fingers.

Teatime echoes
through this pool of shadow.
Butterflies dither
like children's puppets.
White sun settles;
a fan hums dry metal.

A Family In Sepia

They must have been expensive years
for a man still wet behind the ears.
You know he took on her first husband's progeny:
Bessie, Ellen and Dan
whose father, like the lead in a play,
drowned in the canal, 'rescuing a man'.

The father of Herbert, Arthur, May and Lily,
Hilda (my gran), Edith and Billy,
is the patriarch to the left of the middle row.
How could a small town grocer afford the bills
to dress the entire family in the photo
in suits and dresses with such tucks and frills?

Perhaps that's why his eyebrows in fright
are perched, low forehead, about to take flight
parallel with his ample moustache.
Or Great Grandmother sewed them herself I should think,
sat up at night to avoid an eleventh.
Small wonder 'Father' took to drink.

Birtle Dean

At Ellen Hughes's cottage in Birtle,
built of blackened Pennine stone
you'd expect to find stalagmites
growing from the flagstones.
Even the coal fire burned dank like a cellar.
But the privy was overpowered with whitewash
and in the room with elbow chairs
and white lace curtains, the smell of Pears
mingled with paraffin, rock buns cooking
and fuel lamps mellow like olive oil warming.

Gran and I would get off at Jericho
and climb the cobbled street uphill,
holding our breath against the bite
of cotton mills bleaching like ammonia.
Our Auntie Nell would be all dressed up
in a purple costume and lavender hat
that she pronounced 'morve'.
Before being widowed she used to live
at Red Bank House with Uncle Jack
and drive a pony and trap.

The Foreigner

In Waltair it was quite different.
He gave her pearls with the diamond ring.
He was the sort of man who got on with life,
met her, thought she was pretty, wanted to make
love to her and fell into marrying her
when the family was so welcoming.

They were more English than the English
with cut-glass cadences of speech.
Great grandfather was a Christian martyr
who gave up his Brahmin caste and was stoned
while great grandmamma was a maharani
and grandfather wrote a grammatical textbook.

She thought she was a jewel out there,
studying science at Queen Mary's, Madras,
winning the prize at Breeks Memorial
and playing on India Radio.
Here she believed herself to be
a cut above the neighbourhood.

Break-Through

Your tendrils rot, your tentacles blight.
You seep a green shadow of moth-holed might.
I draw my curtains ready for flight.
For once let me break through, stretch your gum,
hang you like washing, bat-winged one,
get out from under your thumb.

These promises, promises unhatched,
have worn me, old record until I'm scratched,
stuck in a groove, detached.
You grind my mind, worm and wheedle.
Your 'Yes' mouth you wear as a beadle.
You've drilled my spine with your needle

until like an empty phial
I've nothing left to spill.

Overlooked

A bird on my lawn
has wings unknown to me.
I look it up in the pocket guide
and find a piece of history.
A page or so back from the cover
the book falls open where my father
placed some four-leaf clover.
Thirty years pressed them further.

He never fails to find whole patches,
around the tartan picnic rug in farmers' gateways.
Egging him on, everyone watches.
He picks one, smiles, a little smug,
holds it up for us to see,
then snaps it into his diary.

To My Father

Today you're like teddy-one-ears
in your brown sweater
with the black diamond markings
torn where it caught on the side-car mudguard.
You're as safe as a deposit box
sharing the day. She
in cotton mill buildings,
their rubber corridors stagnant
with patients' dinners,
collects her soul.

Today we are getting acquainted.
You are not as she said.
I hear you say, 'That's the way.
That was a silly thing to do.
How can we sort it out?'
At the unexpected phone call,
'Run along, enjoy yourself!'
I put on the orange shift dress I made,
cut out, ready to sew from Woman's Realm.
When I go, you don't complain.

Returning I'm bowled over
(finding you still in the garage
tuning the carburettor)
at how your isolation stings me.

Father's Farmyard

Leaves unravel from the earth,
paper parachutes.
Buds, yellow points of sharpened
crayons stand on the brink.
Budding daffodils with necks
like swans, soar into flower.

Frilled in dresses
of tissued crepe paper,
they're too bright
to blow their own trumpets.

My father made a farmyard for my birthday,
painted green fields and loofah hedge
and grew there paper daffodils.

Contained

Tins, the remnants of her birthday.
Emptied of sweets, she kept her belongings in tins.
Patterned, hand-painted enamel, gifts the grandchildren gave
her, she filled with bias binding and lace.

I cannot throw her tins away,
full as she used them with embroidery threads and pins.
I pass her bits and pieces to a dressmaker to save
and look for something to put in their place.

Birthday Present

A lipstick case from my daughter,
a box of daffodil bulbs from my son,
from my husband a bottle of toilet water.
On the mantelpiece are cards from everyone.

At school I'd stake the day as my own
with the date at the top of my paper.
I'd find the table laid at home
with the best serviettes and silver

and my cake all glittering pink and gold.
I smell the candles splutter as they sing.
We were a family of three with lives still untold.
Today my family hold our lives in the making.

Short Vehicle

My world does not close four points down at half-past five
but bright as morning glory, unravels fresh on waking.
The children, powdered and dried from their baths
spill Weetabix on pelican bibs;
spread finger-painting on the oven door;
draw matchstick men and 'eliopcops'
push cars in garage lifts
to roll along the track.

Outside the blue pedal car says on the back:
'Short Vehicle'. Dry days I hang washing on the line,
keeping an eye on the melting space between the gateposts.
Behind the house, the garage-to-be is builders' sand
for buckets, spades and stacking cups to make mud pies.
Evenings, I sweep sand from the drive.
I see the hawthorn hedge, but in my mind:
delphiniums, foxglove, blue iris and cranesbill.

Advent

What with taking a late holiday, November
passed unnoticed in a roller-coaster
of car boot sales, wallpaper stripping,
touching up paintwork and leaf burning.

The weather has held as the corpses
of late bluebottles that shroud our sills
testify. Evidence of further global warming.
Rain stirred in December.

Mornings I'm woken by the post in the hall
or the seven o'clock phone call:
a babel of voices enquiring whether
it's too late to order Lester
Piggott in baby-pink with chocolate spots
while you fire the next batch in your workshop.

Fluorescent light on newsprint after missed lunch
feels like too much rum punch.
Ours remains embryonic on shelves in supermarkets
like mince pies that are figments in packets.

I'm wound up like an optician's duochrome
though you in your work's cocoon
are totally flummoxed by my one error:
banking the Christmas cards with our carrier
of empty bottles, thrown
into holes marked: *clear, green, brown.*

Mother Is Always Right

All in all she left me remarkably unscathed
except in this one attitude.
I remember clearly I believed her.
Mother is always right.

That day she said, 'Happiness is overrated.
Take my advice and don't waste time.
The bluebird has escaped out of the window
and the world may be flat.'

I believed her, only she was wrong.
She taught me that when she died.
With her final note she taught me
that in this life happiness counts like hell.

PEARL M BURDOCK

Much of my life has been spent doing care work in one form or another. I trained as a nursery nurse during my late teens. This involved working in residential orphanages and caring for the unwanted and under-privileged children of the 1950s. After marriage, we soon managed to produce five youngsters of our own.

I continued to do quite a lot of care work while we were raising our family. As they grew up and away, I went to work in a school. This involved introducing physically disabled children into mainstream education. The work was very rewarding to me personally.

I have always been a poet and gained much personal joy through this medium of expression. To be able to touch others through 'written pictures' is a great feeling. I did one creating writing course through evening classes locally, and another through The London School of Writing. This was a home tutorship course.

I have never been a high earner moneywise, this has never bothered me. Work satisfaction is far more important. I like dogs and small animals. Another passion of mine is gardening. I feel this too is very important if we wish to save our beautiful planet for our children and the lives of future generations.

A Taste Of English Heaven

Saddened by the changing faces of our
Sorrowful world, I find tranquillity
Strolling through an old-world village. An hour
. . . or two, of welcome calm, docility
In passing quaint stone cottages. They stand
As splendid reminders of what has been,
A combination of old and new, bland . . .
Yet strong with fertile gardens crisp and clean.
A glass of fine wine amid the locals
At 'The Tavern' before returning home.
The birds are seeking rest from their vocals,
The moon reflecting now, sun's golden comb.

Nostalgic feelings can be forgiven,
Where history kisses English heaven.

A Wee Kiss In The Dark When The Time Is Right

There is a special garden in my mind and also in my heart;
A very special garden, where people who love one
another never part, or hate, or fight or kill.
This very special garden is where all the beautiful
birds have learned to sing and fly. A place where love
will never die.

A place where flowers and shrubs cast out their
beautiful perfume as in prayer. They can be seen,
smelt and touched. Their fragrance lingers in the air,
keeping sweetness in its own abode.

This garden also carries the sight and sound of
children playing in warmth and light-hearted fun.
These are the angels in the garden. Tortoises and
hedgehogs roam in safety. A faithful dog will watch
in fond affection.

Young lovers will pass through, lost in their own ecstasy;
not really noticing what is all around them.
Every so often, the sound of bells will ring out
in joy and beautiful songs and music will fill the air.
This is my dream of Heaven where, one day
I hope I shall abide. I would like to know that
when the time is right, you too will be there
to share God's other kingdom.

Beauty

Bring a little beauty, show someone you care,
Bring a little sunshine where a life seems bare.
Take a tip from nature and little birds that sing,
Putting life and loveliness into everything.
As the years are passing, you will grow in love,
You will find and hold the key to the realms above.

Divine Intervention

Just beneath the surface which,
Right now appears so bare;
There lies a great adventure,
Sleeping sweetly,
Its little roots protected;
Safe in the warmth of the womb.
The womb of our dear Mother Earth;
And soon, old Father Time will give
His nod of approval.
He will breathe his warmth and sweetness
As the sun will pour its rays to warm the Earth.
The seeds and bulbs will blossom,
Hedgerows and trees will rise in sap
And throw their sprigs.
Once again our mother's womb will
Bless us with the incarnation of new
And innocent life.
Our eyes will again see the wonders and
Perfection of divinity.

From Acorns To Oak Trees

From the basic bond of blood-lines - the animated seed
Has rushed amid the flood-lines to nurture and to feed.
A natural propagation secure within its tomb,
Genetic destination provided in the womb.
Then tossed into this big, wide world with kith and kin around,
Like little flags or leaves unfurled - the young will find their ground.
The family will grow with care and blossom at its head,
Then later, so much grief will share, when burying its dead.
So from the simple, tiny spawn - of love and happy mirth,
A fast, dynamic unit forms - the strongest link on Earth.

Forgiving

If rich rewarding harmony is what our lives intend,
We cannot hope to find this unless basically we spend . . .
A part of our lives in understanding fallen brothers,
The need of knowing how to aid and truly help the others.
A genuine desire to make for betterment of Man,
The promise of reality our forefathers began,
The weaknesses of ours as our daily lives we live,
The weaknesses of others and the power to forgive.

Hope And Life

Hope shines from the infants as they gurgle at their mums.
Hope shows through the children as they suck their little thumbs.
Hope glows from the teenagers, filled with life and fun,
Hope is with the parents as they start their work-day run.
Hope lies with the aged as their working life is done,
Hope for the bereaved that a new life has begun.
Hope is for tomorrow as we watch the setting sun,
Hope is breathing essence . . . spurring life in everyone.

Joy In Love

There are many pleasant moments in the course of busy life,
These are often termed as heavenly when not concerned with strife,
Yet the ultimate euphoria, I think you will agree,
Is when couples join together and can live compatibly.
Only fools seek endless paradise, just dreams that fade and die
But to grow in love brings confidence on which each can rely.

In the secret sensuality of sharing in delight,
With love's embers glowing warmly in the middle of the night.
For the giving and the taking, ecstasy you share as one,
Heaven makes its brief appearance giving life before it's gone.
In the rapture of the intimate, enabling you to feel,
The greatest gift from God to Man is pure in love and real.

Miracles

To say there are no miracles would be to tell a lie,
To disregard this wonder would surely make you sigh.
To claim that all is lost and gone to ages long passed by,
Now stop awhile and turn around before you start to cry . . .
To all who have borne children and will do so through the years,
Your miracle has come too when after all the sweat and tears
You hold this tiny being - a replica of love,
Did you not at this moment think of blessings from above?
To others when you wander in a garden or a wood,
Do you not feel and sense a certain power of nature's good?
To those with faith in nothing, then turn towards your heart,
There is something here for everyone but you must find your part.

Patience

The virtue of patient folk has a lesson for us all,
Their quiet, kindly manner in spirit makes them tall.
As tension grips the human race,
The gentle take important place,
Restoring calm to those around,
To help where folk have lost their ground.
Time for understanding could make an end to hate,
Remember . . . also serving is the man who'll stand and wait.

Pride From The Fens

Our garden has no mountains
Or hills for us to climb.
No rich, mysterious fountains
To splash the song of time.
Our lives may look so boring
Within a stranger's view.
We seem forever working
Or waiting in a queue.
Our soil is black with flatlands,
Yet rich in fertile growth.
Our fruit and flowers grow freely
To feed and feast the broth.
We love our little corner
And magic fills our hearts.

To watering mouths our harvest ends
In European parts.

Reflection

A time for reflection,
The chance to recall . . .
Those oh, so special moments,
From the past
That cling to us all.
They give us our background;
They are what we are,
We learn from what has been -
Our prime time, so far.

Our moment in time, here on
Earth is so short. We need
In our hearts to belong
(Need a thought) to grasp . . .
With no greed, just a seed
To hold us together, a clasp
From our past, making now
Very clear. The time for tomorrow
Is *now* and so dear.

Roots In Friendship

Love in friendship has a sweetness of its very own;
Just like the seed of life inside a mother's womb is grown . . .
Developing and taking shape, a life will come to be,
And treasured by the folk around will grow through infancy.
True friendship has a different seed,
Of Faith and Trust is sown.
A fragrance forms and like a prayer
In gentle breeze is blown . . .
Uniting folk in loyalty and love to one another -
The friendship, though no blood is shared
As families with brothers,
Can sometimes mean a great deal more
In loyalty with others.
So often when the troubles in our lives are piling high,
God sends a friend to bear us close and hear us as we cry.

The Kiss Of Spring

A snowdrop shows its pure white head
Above the foliage, dank and dead,
And just a little space away . . .
A primrose casts its pretty spray.
The crocus rises with the rest
And nods its greeting, 'all the best'.
Behind, the hedge of beech, still brown -
In last year's leaves now drooping down . . .
The lawn is kissed in morning dew;
The warming sun delights the queue
Of minutes bringing in the dawn;
A brand new day has just been born.
The birds are singing in full song,
A feathered choir in such sweet throng.
Our Lord, we know is very near . . .
He shows Himself in life so dear.

Thoughts For Our Children

What you have and hope to hold, though proper in its way,
Mortal life at full term is still quite a shortly stay.
Taking stock of basic needs in order to survive,
Add a little luxury to make you feel alive.
Worry not what others have or keeping up the pace,
Much of that just causes stress and lines about your face.
Give yourself a survey, looking deep within your heart,
Check your daily pattern and make sure you play your part.
Spare a thought for others - always let them know you care,
Work out who your friends are - when they need you, just be there.
Do not stoop to jealousy - that is a deadly sin,
Keep your sense of humour - let both light and laughter in.
As you build your empire, you should build your person too,
Also broaden those horizons - that's the vital clue.
Life will be much brighter with a healthy state of mind,
Selfishness will count for less - I know that you will find . . .
A balanced personality that glistens like a star,
It's not what you possess in life, my dears - it's what you are.

RITA CASSIDY

I was born in the north-east, County Durham, in a mining community, and enjoyed the friendliness of neighbouring families. Being aware of life and death issues from a young child, I draw on life experiences, past through to present, for my poems. As I am a Christian, many times I've received inspiration from God and written poems on this particular theme. Also, I do like to write humorously and am experimenting with children's poetry too. I love Creation in all its magnificent forms and try to paint with my pen when inspiration hits me. I cannot decide to write a poem, therefore wherever I'm going, shopping, walking, travelling or talking, I try to make sure paper and pencil are always available. As a few words speed through my brain, a paper hankie or even a cheque book have proved invaluable tools, I find if these few words aren't hastily written down, then for me the plot is lost. I started writing in 1998, a new season of my life emerged as family also left the nest. I enjoy quiet times and found just sitting and writing down my thoughts and feelings helped bring me through some challenging times. I was married young and enjoyed bringing up two sons with my late husband, and moving around the country a few times increased my experiences. Remarrying at the age of 45 years and helping my husband bring up his daughters, meeting them at eight and 13 years, including their girlfriends, we had a large extended family which, of course, included another house move!

Having lived in the Midlands, Kent, Cheshire, Lincolnshire, Norfolk and now West Sussex, many memories I would like to record for my grandchildren in the near future.

Perhaps a novel too?

Remembrance

The poppy bloomed today,
Blood-red.
For five years I had tried to grow
A small plant.
Taken from my father-in-law's garden,
To remind me of him and his dear wife,
So kind, so trustworthy, so loving
To all who knew them.
He was an ambulance man by trade,
Loyal and true with a heart for people.
All during the war years
Dedication to his post,
Through sorrowful times.
A shy man,
Just like my poppy,
Peeping through the undergrowth!
Remembrances so sweet,
Of my dear mother and father-in-law.
He only lived a few months longer than his dear wife.
Their favourite hymn, 'Abide With Me'.

Our Dad

A truly selfless dad was what we had.
A man with a heart as big as his hands.
A man who toiled
In the bowels of the earth.
The overtime he willingly worked
For us, his family,
To give us food and warmth
And a loving home.
Many memories we will have of our dad,
Who had a smile right from his heart.
He blessed many people in his lifetime,
To young and old, many stories he told.
Even going to the mines
His workmates would ask him why he smiled.
His answer was simple, he enjoyed
Every new day that dawned.
His allotment he loved, the sky above,
Hens clucking, rabbits rooting,
Vegetables and flowers in abundance,
All to share, a loving, caring soul was our dad.

The Apple Tree

Oh where can it be
This elusive apple tree,
A friend in dire need
Her instructions to me
To meet her by the apple tree.
We drove round and around
Seemingly glancing at all the trees in Crawley.
Not one was an apple tree,
Then looking up I suddenly saw a sign clearly showing
The apple tree for all to see.
My friend was waving with all her might
Her scarf billowing like a colourful kite.
I didn't admit that I had at last seen the light and found the *pub*
Called 'The Apple Tree'!
Although it was not such a beautiful sight
It was where my friend needed me to be
By, not under, the old apple tree.

Cave

With trepidation we entered the cave,
The dampness shrouding us like a grave.
Shivering we followed the knowledgeable guide.
Obviously her heart was bursting with pride,
As she told us the history in there
Of the last of Ireland's brown bears.
Bones in its lair we saw,
As it wasn't against the law,
For the clearing of the land.
Resulting in plans for roads and homes,
And of course crops to be grown.
Deforestation it's called.
Animals had perished, no habitat left.
Leaving the poor bears bereft.
Then in desperation crawling into
The darkness of their caves,
With waves of desolation.
They laid down and passed away.
Alas the end of the Aillwee bears,
Gone without a care.
Now a tourist attraction
In beautiful County Clare,
To see their lairs.
And as far as I know
They are still there!

Orange

The sun burnt orange in the sky today,
making me want to fly away
to cooler climes, perhaps.
My strength is sapped.
The air hangs heavy and humid,
making even breathing laboured.
Desperate for a shady nook
I look and find refuge in my cool kitchen.
So sad to see that even my little flowers
were frizzling up!
Hot and sticky was the feeling
sending my senses reeling.
Showers only giving temporary relief,
causing me some grief!
Allergic to the sun was my problem,
total sunblock didn't solve
the angry red wheals
that appeared on my neck and arms,
making me feel a total wreck.
Nothing seems to stop this painful itching.
Only my solitary fan helped a little,
indoors, where it was placed.
Making me more determined to make haste,
to buy more!
Because the sun burnt orange in the sky today.
With temperatures rising,
soaring to new heights,
flooring my Englishness,
new records were set in history.
So glad, a few days later
there was no more need to fret.
On looking up I saw clouds moving,
and gentle breezes causing the trees' branches
to sway, promising rain.
Reminding me to give thanks to God,
for a typically English summer's day.

Dawn Kiss

The dawn kisses the Earth,
The Earth awakens,
A new day, a new way to walk,
Opportunities to talk,
To hinder or build up
Our choice.
The tongue can devastate
Like forest fires,
A man can be destroyed
By a wrong word or deed,
God's sunset would not be so beautiful
That day for the hurting soul.
But tomorrow is a new day,
A new way to walk,
Opportunities to talk.
When the dawn kisses the Earth.

The Empty Chair

The chair was old and worn,
battered and torn.
Tobacco-stained with holes burnt into the frame,
fabric marked with spilt tea,
beer and many tears.
Once it was new, with a shiny velvet hue
of gold and brown,
now sad and dejected,
left in a dark corner, bereft of life.
The empty chair,
that was our dad's,
now to be hauled away to the dump,
humped into an old van.
Taking with it a chair full of happy memories.
An old man's refuge.
Seeing a beloved father sitting there,
welcoming, smiling and never complaining.
Through great trials of pain and suffering.
Reminding me that love is patient, love is kind,
love never fails, but love hurts.

Which Way?

Sometimes we walk
With our heads held high,
Sometimes our feet we drag,
Sometimes we linger
And try to recall,
Memories of yesterday
Sorrows and joys,
Laughter and tears,
All past
Yes time goes so fast!
But it is never too late
To walk in God's ways.
Seek and you will find
His mission for your life
But it is your decision!

The Pear Tree

On the banks of the St Lawrence river
Stood a lonely pear tree.
In the garden of a loved one,
A present you see
Given instead of chocolates
A remembrance from me,
Of a visit enjoyed.
In the years to come yielding fruit,
I hoped.
But I hadn't reckoned a tree
So lonely
Could not produce fruit.
In God's plan it would take
A male and female pear tree
To produce delicious fruit.
Then six years later, just in time,
A miracle happened, pollination
Through some little busy bees,
A pear tree must have been planted
In a neighbouring garden, because
The year 2000 yielded the lonely trees
First harvest of delicious pears!
I was so glad
As the barren pear tree was to
Have been chopped down,
And discarded as useless
Of which I felt very sad,
But God knew!

Extinct

Where has it gone?
No more to see
A place of friendliness for me
Somewhere to go to meet friend or foe,
Alas now extinct like the poor dodo.
What can we do?
When the giants have stampeded in,
Selling everything
Including the kitchen sink.
Prices slashed, no more trash.
Even fruit has to be the right shape,
For goodness sake, I stand aghast!
And what a shock at the till I find.
My budget over the years has climbed and climbed.
No more as careful as our parents were,
Temptation to buy and try, delights our eye.
Bright packaging that we cannot eat.
It's just that as human beings,
We're always looking for a treat.
The corner shop has disappeared
From our day-to-day living.
For we have voted with our feet,
Also causing the corner shops to retreat.

Senior Moment

It was a senior moment
Just to coin a phrase
It should have been a great time
Jumping on and off the bus
Such an adrenaline rush.
I'd already returned home
At a leisurely pace
Now I'm once again in the race
To find a missing bag
What a fag!
What should I do, I need a clue.
Backtracking my mind
Hoping to find
The missing bag,
Alas rushing again to catch the bus,
Feeling hot and very nonplussed
Wishing the ride would quicken up!
Charity shops here I come
But in one I was to become undone
A bag stolen was my plight
I must have looked an awful sight
The answer from everyone
Was sorry but no info.
So here I go, home again,
Feeling like a defeated foe.
I walked the final steps,
A brainwave, surely there was
One place, I hadn't checked well,
I raced upstairs, and there behind the door
An answer to my prayers.
The missing bag full of toys
Placed, now traced.
Facing the facts.
A senior moment, what a laugh
Merriment is so good for the heart
Perhaps now I can enjoy
A cup of tea and two jam tarts!

ZOLTAN P DIENES

My life spans the years between the collapse of the Austria-Hungarian monarchy and our attempts to reach Mars. My early years were spent in Hungary, Austria, Italy and France.

As a result of the collapse, finally opting for England at the age of fifteen, I studied mathematics at the University of London. I later became more interested in the problems of learning mathematics than in creating new mathematics. I spent the first decade or so of my professional life in teaching and creating mathematics, mostly at universities, but from the later fifties on I used my time in exploring what could be done to improve the scandalously low standard of mathematics teaching all over the world. To this end I worked in Leicester (England), Adelaide (Australia), Lae, Mount Hagen (New Guinea), New York, Palo, Alto, Minneapolis (USA), Sherbrooke (Quebec, Canada), Brandon (Manitoba, Canada), Frankfurt (Germany), Florence, Cosenza (Italy), Porto Alegre (Brazil) and several other places, researching in theoretical and practical ways to try to solve the many problems. I have published papers and written books through which I have tried to help the process along. Some mathematical games which are fun to play can be found on my website www.zoltandienes.com.

My wife Tessa (1920-2006) and I became friendly during our teens (although we had already met when she was only ten), the friendship being entirely platonic for a number of years. In the end nature spoke and we fell in love, married and had a family of five children.

As I was winding down my professional work as an octogenarian, I began to think that the medium of poetry could be yet another vehicle for transmitting ideas. To put this into practice I have tended to use a rather strict meter and rhyme structure, thus bucking the modern trend for 'freedom'; I suppose I could not really silence the mathematician in me.

I dedicate this part of the volume to my wife and five children.

The Wednesday Shopping

Every Wednesday at Save-Easy there's a discount: five percent,
Just as long as you're a senior and a good sum you have spent.
I believe it's twenty dollars that this sum has got to be,
But it can be more than twenty, more to spend you're always free!

There is parking for us seniors a few metres from the door
So we do not have to walk far, which for seniors is a bore!
So we take a shopping carriage which are waiting to be picked
We've the list of what we're short of, with each item to be ticked.

Our first stop is at the milk shelf where we look at every bag
And we search for all the latest, though we can't read every tag!
Milk and yoghurt must be fat-free or at most just one per cent,
Cream and such like, as we're seniors, in our health might make a dent.

When we look at all the cheeses, some are tasty, some are fat,
If we get some parmeggiano, I will surely eat my hat!
It does seem we've run the gauntlet of the foods with too much fat,
So we now go to the fruit shelves and declare that that is that!

All the fruit is too expensive, all excepting berries blue,
So blueberries are for breakfast or some plums might have to do!
Now the greens are for perusal, look! the cabbage is so cheap!
Broccoli is too expensive, prices up and up do leap!

Now we've toured the entire system, checking out is now what's next,
Credit card is what we need now, if it's lost we shall be vexed.
Of the purse we search the content, it's our luck, our card is there!
With this card we do get air-miles, so we can fly everywhere!

Then the girl who's at the checkpoint calls a young man to our aid,
Who will help us take the shopping to the car when all is paid.
When we're home there will be Sarah to unload what we have bought
As we can't do too much lifting or we would be brought to naught!

Leslie's Birthday

Last week it was Leslie's birthday, so we asked her round to tea,
We asked Bruce and Gwen to come too, it was lucky they were free.
And our grandson we invited, from Australia, just returned,
He'd amuse us with his stories, telling things that he had learned.

With the jelly made by Sarah and two cakes that Tessa made,
We did welcome our invited with whom we would celebrate.
Eighty candles were too many, eight and zero, they would do
For the singing of the greeting, 'Happy birthday here to you!'

With one candle on the zero and another on the eight
Showed that she's lived eighty years now, and this we must celebrate!
Leslie did have just enough breath to blow out her candles two
So we did congratulate her, she had known just what to do!

Leslie is a chiropractor, she has mended many backs,
In this delicate procedure there are certainly some knacks!
She's the kind that works quite gently, with no cracking of the neck,
Those that use the cracking method often leave you quite a wreck!

How Tessa And I Keep Going

(Back to elongated anapaests)

When you get into your eighties, you must see your doctor often,
With pneumonia on the doorstep, do be careful with the coughing!
See your doctor every four weeks
(though you'd want to go more often).
Doctors have a busy schedule. It's unlikely that they'll soften!

In your blood the pressure's rising, or it might be getting low;
Is this due to medications? Or are all things *comme il faut?*
Use the puffer for the breathing, mind you breathe in and then out
So whatever's in the puffer gives your lungs a lot more clout!

For your heart you'll take the hawthorn as you've had a heart attack,
Even though your heart is damaged, this makes up for any lack.
Carnatine and Leonarius, they are added to the brew,
Making things much more effective, it's the best thing you can do!

Lois is your naturopractor, you consult her on the phone,
She is sure to reassure you, so you will not feel alone.
Every two months you go see her and she'll check out how you are.
Pity she lives down in Berwick, to go often it's too far!

When you feel the need is urgent, there's a clinic down the road,
There's a doctor there on duty and it's quite near our abode.
They can check on all your functions so that you can feel at rest,
And you'll get expert instructions from the doctors who know best!

Ranidine and diuretics by the doctors are prescribed
Astrogalus must be added, if it's nature that's your guide!
In your vessels plaques are growing, for this enzymes you must take,
Enzymes or an operation! That's the choice that you must make.

You must try to keep the balance twixt convention and the new
Using only naturopathic is a risky thing to do!
If no studies with control groups have been done for certain things
It might happen that your illness, you'll exchange for angels' wings!

The Driving Test

It is getting problematic if I should still drive the car,
All the time I'm getting older and I can't drive very far!
Then one day I got a notice for an oldies' driving test,
Someone thought, if I stopped driving, on the whole it would be best!

When the date was fixed for testing, I called on one driving school,
Some good lessons would be useful, failing test would not be cool!
The instructor took me round on all the circuits of the test,
He corrected some bad habits, for his patience he'll be blessed!

When the test came I was ready to show off my new-found skill,
I did think I knew the tricks now, so I hoped I'd foot the bill!
Shoulder checks I had forgotten every time I made a turn
But I had not done too badly, sure my licence I would earn!

When at last the test was over, my good tester said to me:
'You have just scraped through the test! Man! One solution I can see!
You can keep your driving licence but in town you must remain,
Though you can drive in bad weather, in the snow or pouring rain!

I'll change nothing in your licence but you will be honour bound
To remain in city limits, so just do your daily round!'
'I do give my word of honour that I'll do as you do say
Regulations? I might break them! But my honour, in no way!'

He did also make me promise that I'd back into my drive,
So for leaving I'd face forward, every time that I arrive.
I have kept my word of honour, I reverse in every time,
Never back into the road now, even though it's not a crime!

In the town of Greater Wolfville, service stations are now closed,
How do I now get our petrol, if in town I am enclosed?
I can ask my son or grandson to be driving to the pumps,
These are out of city limits, but my conscience gets no lumps!

Problems Of Helping The Old

We do have our youngest daughter living with us in our home,
Which occasions some adjustments as I'll tell you in this poem:
How can those still in their fifties live with those of eighty plus?
If one can't find a solution, somewhere someone's missed the bus!

Don't forget we were created by a God who is all-wise,
So to Him we take our problems, He will surely hear our cries!
When approaching hundred years of life, lived here on this good Earth,
Day to day we must be thinking: of what care we are still worth?

How the people in their fifties do decide to fill their days,
Must be left for their decision, which could go in many ways!
If we oldies need assistance which implies great gifts of time,
We must sometimes give it up for to assist those in their prime!

Two old people find it hard for one another to assist,
Giving service during night-time is so often on the list
Cups of tea or some bed-warmers could be needed right at dawn
So you rise and do this service and don't leave your spouse forlorn!

Such commotion, our dear daughter, it does wake her from her sleep,
Which because of heavy duties, had become so very deep!
'I will cope with this new problem!' says she to her tired dad,
She takes over from her father, who thinks this is not so bad!

She's web-master of web-Alpha for Canadians organised,
It's important that web-users of new ventures be apprised!
When the need for helping parents with such work it does conflict,
'Shall I help? Or the computer to web-Alpha should have clicked?'

She does think that she must have one job that is her very own,
What she gets from her old parents, she regards as just a loan.
She does like to have the feeling that her pay is truly earned
If she opts for restaurant work, we should not be too concerned.

We cannot ourselves decide on other people's moral code
How can we adjudicate on what for them is the right road?
If a friend's act's not convenient, it does not mean that it's wrong,
Toleration is the keyword, so we all can get along!

ZOLTAN P DIENES

The End Of A Road

There's a crisis in the offing, we can feel it right inside,
Tessa's speaking rather strangely, she her feelings cannot hide;
It's her heart that's getting weaker since she had her heart attack,
Sure that time is marching on and we just cannot turn it back!

Her poor heart, her blood is pumping but it can't pump fast enough,
So her legs are badly swelling, they appear to be so rough!
To the hospital she's taken as the danger is quite clear,
So some quick help from the doctors should always be very near.

Intravenous diuretic makes the swelling go right down,
She receives the best attention that's available in town.
She receives some telephone calls from her friends around the world,
She is pleased with the attention and she soaks in every word.

Two days pass and she is cheerful and all think she's on the mend,
She is able on the phone now cheerful messages to send.
Soon there comes a sudden change as just to breathe becomes too hard,
While her heartbeat's getting slower, putting doctors on their guard.

Then her heart stops, having beaten very well since it began,
And the doctors caring for her, they try everything they can.
But it seems her time has come and there is nothing more to do,
God has called her to be with Him and His call, it must be true!

I am on my way to see her, to the hospital we drive,
And we go up to her quarters just as soon as we arrive.
In her room there's much commotion with the doctors all around,
But from Tessa there is quiet, she can utter no more sound!

We are just too late to see her in her body of this life,
But I kiss her lifeless body, which contained my darling wife;
We sit with her in the silence and we hope her soul can hear
That I am forever with her, still remaining very near.

This goodbye is not forever, up above we'll meet again,
In a new life filled with love which just for now's beyond my ken.
Sixty-eight years lived together is a priceless gift to me,
For this treasure I've been granted, to God thankful I must be!

Tessa's Burial

On the twenty-first of this month, her last journey, it was planned,
No event could have been sadder if my whole life I had scanned!
Her expression was so peaceful as she lay there in her box,
I could hardly dare to touch her and disturb her curly locks!

They were there, her son and daughters though the eldest was away,
She was not allowed to travel so in England she did stay.
The good Baptists and the Quakers for the service did unite
For my dearest wife departed, they composed a Holy rite.

Clarinet quintet was played as it was played some weeks ago
At my birthday celebration and dear Tessa loved it so!
Then we heard a lot of stories of my dear wife's loving acts,
Many had tears in their eyes as they related all these facts!

At the end I kissed her forehead ere the casket's lid was shut,
She was carried to the grave, which of the service was the cut.
We all had some tea and cake before we followed to the grave,
Standing there, we sang her best hymns and I did try to be brave!

She was lowered in the grave and we did sadly say goodbye,
Thus did end a weighty chapter with no eyes remaining dry.
Two grandchildren and three children of my dear wife they came home,
And our feelings felt together, would have filled a heavy tome!

Living Without Tessa
(Part 1)

When I feel sad I get my pen and my sad thoughts try to write
Deep in my soul I seek the Christ and my despair try to fight.
I do recall the precious times that Tess and I always shared
When every moment that we lived was a great gift, since we cared.

During each night I shared with you I placed my hand on your side
You'd hold my hand and hold it tight as would befit a young bride!
In all we felt we were as one and we thanked God for this love,
Its precious gift from our Lord God in this sad world, from above.

My precious love! You are not here when I seek you during the night!
But I do hope you are surrounded where you are, by God's own light!
The lovely garden that you'd seen some days before you passed away
It must have been a sign from God that your dear soul was on its way!

Now every day when I do wake I still make tea for you and me,
The second cup I drink for you just as before it used to be!
Your little towel I can still touch, that you did use on your dear chest,
Then I lie back on our big bed, so I can have another rest.

Thus getting used to life without you, it will certainly be hard,
All the time things you did for me recovery will now retard!
If I'd passed on before you did, it would have been too hard for you,
But the way God had it ordained, I must work out what I can do!

Living Without Tessa
(Part 2)

In the morning when I wake, now I'm aware that I'm alone,
It does hit me with its harshness and it chills me to the bone.
We were always close together, a whole lifetime we have spent
With each other in all weathers and your death my heart has rent!

You would want me not to break down in this crisis of my life,
So I'll try to carry on now notwithstanding all the strife!
There might still be in this life some further useful things to do
Though I'll always be remaining in my love joined onto you.

I do hope that your dear soul, it has now found a lovely place,
Free of tears and apprehensions and surrounded by God's grace.
It cannot now be too long before we two can meet again
In the next mode of existence where we suffer no more pain!

Tessa, dearest! I must thank you for the things you did for me;
I do miss your kind reminders and our frequent cups of tea!
All your friends keep telling stories of how kind to them you've been,
A more generous, lovely person they had never, never seen!

This is not a goodbye message, au revoir it has to be!
Up above we'll be united: an eternal you and me!
Sixty-eight years life together is our gift from our good Lord,
I will thank Him for His caring by the reading of His word!

Even The Cat Takes Part In The Grief

On Saturday we went to Bruce's house
Which much emotion in me did arouse;
It is a place where we've spent happy days,
Where of the sun, we've watched the setting rays!

Bruce was about to stack the winter's wood,
This is hard work: it must be understood!
Our grandson Dan, we asked the work to share,
He's always there to help, which is so rare!

I was supplied with protein drink and pie
Before my rest, when on the couch I'd lie,
The others then the stacking, they would start
To finish while it's light, which was so smart!

Our Bruce and Gwen do have a wondrous cat
(Although he seems a little bit too fat!)
He seems quite keen to share what humans feel,
In some strange way, their sadness tries to heal!

When I'd lain on the couch to have my rest,
This cat came up and snuggled on my chest!
He stayed with me while I was fast asleep
And silently my company did keep.

Most cats don't know of logic and long words,
Their song is not quite up to that of birds,
Beyond all words and songs they have a sense
To know a way to make one feel less tense!

This cat, he must have felt the pain in me,
It was with me that he did wish to be!
The spirit that surrounds us all was there
Uniting Man and beast in loving care!

ANDREW FARMER

The survivor of twin boys born in July 1939, was raised and schooled in Fife during its mining heyday. A degree at Edinburgh University, and marriage to Freda in 1962, saw him embark upon a science teaching career which began in Kirkcaldy (Fife) and ended in Norwich (Norfolk) in 1990, by early retirement on medical grounds. Andrew is registered as blind.

Freda and he have raised three children viz Jacqueline, born 1964, Peter born 1965, and Richard born 1972. Jacqueline has Down's Syndrome.

Sadly, the tenor of life within an innately happy family was adversely transformed by a sequence of traumatic events involving each of the now adult children in turn.

In 1984 Peter was seriously injured and incapacitated in a car accident. He still lives at home with his parents.

Then in 1992, whilst in residential care, Jacqueline had a breakdown, subsequently diagnosed as Post Traumatic Stress Disorder (PTSD), which resulted in a hospital stay of ten years. During therapy she alleged serious abuse at the hands of a named male carer. She is now back in community care. And then, tragically, presumably as the consequence of trying to cope with a lengthy troubled relationship - which did produce a gorgeous little son - Richard, aged 29 years, committed suicide. Andrew and Freda are now denied access to their grandson and have little contact with his maternal half of a family.

Andrew has written poetry since the early 1980's, has self-published five books about his own coalmining roots, and his more recent family situation.

The present compilation offered here contains a balanced mix of old and new, past events and recent experiences, which between them, reflect the most important issues in Andrew's personal and family life.

His long-term favourite poet is Philip Larkin. John Betjeman runs a close second.

When Dame Fortune Did Smile

White-hatted, neat in a pleated
Suit of blue, relaxing, she sat
Upon grass in Princes Street gardens,
The cragginess of Edinburgh's castle
Softened by a touch of warm
Afternoon sun, and by the spontaneity
Of her smile, expressing a happiness
To treasure, a moment of real pleasure,
Fortuitously, forever preserved on film.

Almost from that one precious shared moment
In time, our disparate lives soon began
To more intimately intertwine, to coalesce
Into an intense and loving wedded consummation,
And a future together which her hands
Helped fashion, using the same gentle
Sureness of touch once captured by camera,
When my heart was touched by her smile,
All those so very happy forty-five years before.

Seeing Eye To Eye

Here I am again,
A genuine VIP,
Registered as blind,
Come for another consultation,
Bringing along with me
As always, the object
Of interest and concern,
My flawed right eye,
Already bracing itself
Against invasion by medication.
Drops to dilate or placate,
And to facilitate proper examination
By lens and by lights
Bright enough to illuminate
What lies hidden inside,
But now made visible
To those who know,
Experts on the retina,
The macula, the cornea,
Consultants most learned
In the field of optometry,
Each with the time
To stand and stare, to ponder,
And to look at me
In the eye.

Back From The Brink

Away back in '92, she consistently
Alleged serious abuse by a carer,
Describing assaults cruel enough
To have damaged her mind
Almost beyond psychiatric repair.

'That man is inside my head,'
She'd said, an uncannily astute
Attempt at self-diagnosis that astounded
Attendant professionals, who'd judged
Such insights, well beyond her.

For her particular learning disability
Is chromosomal, she has Down's Syndrome,
A genetic jigsaw grown askew,
In which just one extra piece
Has so adversely distorted her capacities.

And yet, after years of hospitalisation,
Coupled with therapy and counselling
Appropriate to her anguished mental state,
She has now braved Community Care anew,
Her trust in people virtually restored.

Lamping The Flame

Hugging the roof spaces,
Hovering unseen,
Lurks hellfire itself,
Predating the cloven face
For incautious Man,
And his dancing naked flame.

For no light of day
Could breach that total dark,
Scores of fathom below,
To show just where
Virgin coal seams lay,
Waiting to be stripped bare.

And so such nakedness
Had to be sheathed,
To screen out heat from light,
And by inhibiting full consummation
Between firedamp and flame,
The Davy lamp saved lives.

Roof Fall

Sometimes Death descended like a hawk
Swooping upon unsuspecting prey,
Thousands of feet below in the dark,
As a sudden shift in the clay
Loosed tons of coal onto unprotected backs.

Up above, the living held their breath
And tried not to readily succumb
To ever present fears, as news from beneath
Confirmed some men had died, their tomb
A rock-strewn shroud of unforgiving earth.

Much later, a respectful silence reigned
Behind drawn blinds, as bereaved spouses
Mourned, and as their grief spread
By word of mouth, in some other houses
Couples moved closer together in bed.

Picket

Was yesterday just some dreadful dream,
Or was that nightmarish scene
Real, the fighting, the violence, a scream
That was mine, the terrible searing
Pain, a police horse, frightened, rearing,
Bruising my back, rupturing my spleen?

Fear is no stranger to a mine,
Yet, cold shivers caress my spine
Recalling the menace of that broad blue line,
A wedge, a concentration of beef and brawn,
Truncheoned, acting out a role, uniformed pawns
Dancing to a ruthless political tune.

Out To Grass

Crows chattering in the treetops
Overhead, a babble on the branches,
Contrasts starkly with his stillness,
A solitary figure, cropping grass,
Munching ruminatively in his own
Little corner of a fenced meadow.

Unlike the cackling black carrion
Up above, he has longevity,
And a past that resides within him
Still, in his bowed over-taxed
Frame, his dust-matted mane,
And the damaged unseeing eyes.

Despite the freedom to graze
Unconfined, he moves around by touch,
And scent, nuzzling for sweet clover
Among the host of wild flower,
For he sees little more than before,
Whilst working below, hauling hutches of ore.

Sharing stable space with scuttling mice,
Caged canaries, and flies that swarmed
In the lamp lights of miners cutting coal
From face, harnessing equine power to move
It from there to elsewhere, a union
Of labours in an era now long gone.

Missing You

There is now
This awful emptiness
In our lives,
An unfillable space
Where you used to be,
The last born,
Indeed always the baby
Of our family of three.

My son, why did you
Take your leave
So very suddenly
From those who grieve,
Bereft and heartbroken,
Mourning a loss
Impossible to replace,
Almost too difficult to bear?

Fortunately we have memories,
Those affectionate hugs now
Never to be, that shy smile
We won't ever see,
A rich legacy of love
That overwhelms yet sustains,
A symptom of grief,
An antidote to pain.

ANDREW FARMER

Nothing More To Say

A wall,
Not just any wall,
But one sea-breezed,
Stout built, and a listed
Artefact of Norfolk history
Up Waxham way.

Which she, mother of his child,
Had said, much later,
He'd use if things got too much
For him to bear,
Which they did do,
Tragically, in May 2002.

And if she'd said it, sooner,
To those who really cared,
Perhaps he'd still be here,
Her child need not have lost
His loving father, and we
Would not have lost a son.

Something Evil Comes This Way

Sent to us
With malicious intent,
On the very morning
Of the formal inquest
Into our son's sudden
And very unexpected suicide,
It slithered through our letterbox,
Packaged, anonymous, yet addressed
With a pen poisonous enough
To paralyse human sensibilities
On such a day, and written
In a hand we recognised.

Alas, there was no antidote
To thirty sheets of religious toxin,
Each a page of scripted nonsense
Evangelising the misguided dogma of Jehovah,
Other than to hold such material,
And its sender, in absolute disdain.

Its despatch to us, just then,
Was indeed a wicked act,
One motivated by vindictiveness,
A wish to intimidate,
And a maternal possessiveness
Fast growing out of control.

Like Father, Like Son

My son,
You were the family face,
A true composite of forbears,
Of familiars, like me,
Or grandad, and others
You were too young to know.

> Features and characteristics
> Defined as of old,
> In profile, or smile,
> Or colour and boldness of eye,
> Reflecting past generations long gone,
> And lives left largely untold.

Yet, old genes were reborn
As if new,
Transcending our mere mortality
And time flown,
To be recast in a uniqueness
That was you.

> And now, despite your tragic
> Very premature demise,
> That heredity has not died,
> For within that gorgeous little son
> Of your own,
> An essence of family lives on.

Bridging Troubled Waters

My dearest grandson,
Although little can be done
To remedy the contact situation
Now grown between us following
The tragic loss of your father,
Back in May 2002,
Please be assured
That your paternal heredity
Remains very secure, and free
To emerge unscathed one day
For everyone to see,
Since you too have inherited
The Farmer face that we,
Your late father and me,
Also embrace, and as three
Branches of the same family tree,
We have both an ancestry
And a proud pedigree to share.

ANDREW FARMER

Elixir Of Life

Memories,
My dear friend,
Like old photographs
Or good verse,
Are timeless,
And as portraits
In the attic
Of the mind,
Are ageless
As Dorian Gray,
Preserving youthfulness
Almost indefinitely,
Until, like shadows
In light that is dying,
We ourselves,
In turn,
Become the remembered,
The fond memory.

KEN LOU

Can a poem be an ambassador of peace, an instrument for international understanding? If one verse can touch one heart, it may open a window for one person to see our planet in a different light. When we help initiate a caring global community, a day will come when pain and hatred slowly fade away, even though it is ever so slowly. Poems of conscience in simple language. Words of common usage, familiar to people from diverse backgrounds. Commonplace expressions presented in a manner ordinary folks are comfortable with. Saying it as it is, in all seriousness, for those who refrain from doing so out of fear or uncertainty. Plainly spoken, with good humour. Reader-friendly, recitable verses that are easy to remember. One word, one verse becomes a catalyst that starts a moment of contemplation, a kind action.

These poems draw inspiration from two personal acquaintances, a past Life that has been most gracious and old friend Death, who must come calling again one last time. I am grateful for the timeless glory of the Italian Renaissance, the tireless spirit of science and the endless courage of those selfless ones who ask for no reward. World wars begin from wounded minds. A trivial incident can lead to a huge misunderstanding. When we put aside our fears and stop the self-persecution, we remove fences and set our hearts free. We have one life in this lifetime, one chance to do the right thing before we go. There is so much yet to be done before our time is over. Let the children inherit a kinder world.

If one poem can bring a smile and make one child happy . . .

The War Within

Humankind has gone through many battles, warfare has a long history,
But there's another kind of battle, a war that's inside you and me,
We punish those who steal our possessions, are we ourselves innocent?
We condemn those who question our beliefs, shouldn't we be
more tolerant?
We denounce those who subvert our culture, don't we too defile others?
We curse those who commit terrorism, have we not killed our
own brothers?
Making use of people to serve our gains, we exploit and dominate,
Absolving ourselves of our own misdeeds, we betray and castigate,
Taking revenge on those who did us wrong, we scheme to level
the scores
And when friends become mortal enemies, aren't we waging
our own wars?
Can we question our social values and listen to honest reason?
Can we live with our bitter memories, stop the self-persecution?
Can we stand up for our past mistakes and overcome our
biggest fears?
Can we face up to those we hate, that hatred we've built up all
these years?
Shaping the world to our convenience, we crave for power and profit,
Claiming divine cause for our actions, we yearn for reward and credit,
Envying those who are better off, we're jealous because they have more
And when we become our worst enemy, we're our own prisoners
of war.
When we welcome contentment, love and peace, there's self-liberation,
When we pacify anger with kindness, it's the end of aggression,
When we forgive those who have harmed us, it's the start
of a new day,
When we begin to respect and care, hatred will slowly fall away.
Each of us has a constant battle, a choice between virtue and sin,
While we're fighting for a better world, the real war, is the war within.

KEN LOU

Twa Pints O' Heavy

Grandmother's Knee, ghost stories over Radio Four,
Great Western Road, freshly fallen snow,
The changing seasons of serene Kelvingrove Park,
And the *bonnie, bonnie* streets of dear Glasgow.

Discovering the scenic beauty of Scotland,
Hearing about the Loch Ness Monster,
Reading up on the folklore of Celtic history,
Experiencing the fame of British weather!

Charles Rennie Mackintosh, the Glasgow School of Art,
Renfrew Street, number one-six-seven,
Prof Andy's lunchtime lecture, *twa pints o' heavy*,
Old Fred, historian, *Battleship Potemkin!*

Brave Ewart on his trusty bike, come snow or sleet,
Wee Becky, she kicked a mean football,
Mad Willie, missing classes for nine holes of golf,
High-spirited classmates, twenty-eight in all.

Strolling along the sidewalks of Sauchiehall Street,
Munching on a salty old *bridie*,
Digesting classic movies at the *GFT*,
Cracking up over big Billy Connolly!

The fire at Grosvenor Hotel late one afternoon,
Sudden hailstorms in the summer heat,
Unforgettable memories, tales yet untold,
That ghost in our student house at Hillhead Street!

Camping by the enchanting shores of Loch Lomond,
Breathing the essence of highland pride,
Feeling the rapture, hill-walking in *Scottish Mist*,
Recalling those good times by the River Clyde.

The Greatest Gift

Who remembers you as a wee baby?
Cleaned you up when you got really dirty?
Busily working while you were sound asleep,
When you were just a tiny little heap.

Forgiving when you didn't do as you were told,
Keeping you warm when the weather was cold,
Feeding you more when you hadn't had your fill,
Taking good care of you when you fell ill.

Who will be there no matter what you do?
Those comforts she will forgo just for you,
Bearing the faults you've yet to confess
Even after you've made a complete mess!

No reward is too small, no pain too much,
An unbreakable bond, that caring touch,
Your sadness is her grief, your bliss, her joy,
Her child is her life, be it girl or boy.

Teaching a little mind to learn new things,
Teaching a little bird how to use its wings,
The greatest gift from the heavens above,
The greatest love, is our mother's love.

Soggy Potato Chips

Not having been to Karl Marx's grave, Highgate Cemetery,
Regrets there were some, though far in-between,
Jeremy Bentham, embalmed, sitting in his cabinet?
There are always some things, best left unseen.

Carnaby Street, Oxford Street and Number 10 Downing Street,
It's been many years since leaving Heathrow,
Although I'm no longer there, my heart still remembers,
That little London town I used to know.

Sangey from Bhutan, George from Greece, Katia from Sicily,
And Kitty from Mobile, Alabama,
Chris from Hong Kong, Kumar from Fiji, Abdel from Kuwait,
And of course, Taina from Finland, Taina.

The delicious *shish kebab* along Tottenham Court Road,
That good old pub at every street corner,
Queuing up for English *fish and soggy potato chips*,
And finishing with a pint of lager!

The lovely humanity on Sundays at Camden Lock
The Egyptian Gallery, British Museum,
That Carnival fever, on the pavements of Notting Hill
Stargazing, at London Planetarium.

Catching the latest scandals on *Not The 9 o'clock News!*
Dollar Brand, *live*, at the Student Union,
Not missing *The Professionals* after *Top of the Pops!*
Our Boy George, and his *Karma Kameleon.*

Those imposing chimneys of Battersea Power Station,
The awesome power of the Thames Barrier,
That age-old chime of Big Ben, reminding us where we were,
A long time past, yet it is still so clear.

Grandmother's Tail

A long time ago, when night was longer than day,
In the deep, deep forest, so very far away,
A fierce old tigress, living out her twilight years,
She had spilled much blood and her heart could shed no tears.

Moonlight was fading, old bones so tired and weak,
Teeth had become blunt and her feet no longer quick,
Look for easy meat that will not put up a fight?
Those ones with two legs and their taste was sheer delight!

When the deed was done, licking her blood-tainted paws,
Not a morsel left and the flavour in her claws,
Walking on two feet, her body no longer frail,
A new lease of life and a cunning, twitching tail!

Can you hear her roar in your childhood memory?
On a cold dark night and sitting at Grandma's knee,
Is there such monster that can take a human form?
Move without a sound and a voice like raging storm!

Even to this day, she is still crunching her bone,
Old tigress lives on and her heart harder than stone,
Story goes like this as they always tell you so,
Not very far away and only a while ago.

She Rules With Grace

Loved by kind folk, big and small,
She is known to one and all,
Calm and cool, she has a style,
The whole world has seen that smile,
A light to all, creed or race,
Then and now, she rules with grace.

Keep the faith and speak with pride,
Spread the good word, far and wide,
This day, the day of her birth,
It is time, for joy and mirth,
Make your wish and raise a cheer,
Say it soft but say it clear,

It will be, as it has been,
All hearts join to bless, The Queen.

Legacy

The British Isles has given us many treasures,
It has produced famous historical figures,
Brave, heroic women of substance,
Noble gentlemen of eminence,
They've touched our lives in many ways, over the years.

The Pink Panther, Mr Bean, the Loch Ness Monster!
Kenneth Williams, 'carrying on up the Khyber!',
Laughing it out with Monty Python,
Giving peace a chance with John Lennon
And of course, everyone's scared of Margaret Thatcher!

Stonehenge, that ancient stone circle, Wiltshire county,
Salisbury Cathedral, classical antiquity,
Windsor Castle, Hampton Court Palace,
Westminster, Piccadilly Circus,
Stratford-upon-Avon, William Shakespeare country.

Christopher Lee and his Hammer House of Horror!
Crafty Sherlock Holmes and the Sussex Vampire!
Agatha Christie, Humpty Dumpty,
Jane Austen, James Bond, Sean Connery,
Battle of Britain, *Supermarine Spitfire!*

Since that very first voyage of discovery,
The British have left a wonderful legacy,
An international language,
An unforgettable heritage,
Mother Earth is thankful to have this great country.

From the Mull of Kintyre to the White Cliffs of Dover!
From misty Scottish Highlands to the Yorkshire Moor!
Walter Scott, Rob Roy McGregor,
Robin Hood, sweet Lady Godiva,
And long shall live the legend of good King Arthur!

Getting There

You know that you're really getting old,
When you talk like you're giving a sermon,
What looks like dead skin turns out to be mould
And a slow walk feels like a marathon!

When you creak out of bed in the morning,
Everything smells worse than the day before,
All your bones and ligaments are aching,
While you keep discovering a new sore!

Crossing the road is a major event,
Every song you sing is out of tune,
Folks rush up to help when you start to pant,
Folks walk off whenever you start to croon!

You forget what you've just been saying,
Cannot remember what you had for lunch,
Half a flight of stairs will leave you gasping
And intoxication has lost its punch.

Sitting in that old chair counting your years,
Wearing the same old clothes for days on end,
Finding new cavities in your dentures,
Forgetting the name of your closest friend.

Things you hate to do, things you just couldn't,
Come so easily even if you wouldn't,
Things you love to do, things that you shouldn't,
No matter how hard you try, you just couldn't.

And when you retire in the evening,
To unload your body parts, one by one,
Just think, if life on Earth was a blessing,
Won't life in Heaven be even more fun?

The Giant's Graveyard

There is talk of a sighing creek, of which local folks dread to speak,
Its dark waters are cold and still, rolling mist brings a sudden chill,
When time is ancient history, where nameless river meets the sea?
That's the place the giants sleep, behemoths and phantoms of the deep.

Step onboard for an hour's ride, they leave nine sharp from the
harbour-side,
The weather clears, the sun shines through, river mouth gleaming
green and blue,
Forest and rock walls here and there, peace and quiet everywhere,
But as the boat turns round the bend, you know you've come to
journey's end.

Words alone may not suffice, the scene that opens before your eyes,
Ships and ships standing side by side, swaying gently with silent tide,
Creaking and rusting mast to keel, towering giants of weathered steel,
Machines that had run out of date, empty shells awaiting their fate.

And on a grey and dreary day, one more draws near in grim decay,
Battered hunk of mighty girth, coming wearily to claim its berth,
Sounding an old horn past its prime, dropping its anchor one last time,
Another ship has come to die, a final painful, desperate sigh.

Crew and captain have gone at last, sea-faring days are long, long past,
Others come to take their place, those that disappeared without a trace,
Returning to their destiny, ghosts of sailors who died at sea,
Back to ships that gave their best, together they find eternal rest.

Sometimes on dark and stormy nights, you may see strange
mysterious lights,
Sighing voices echoing in waves, spectral ships rising from their graves,
Witness to deeds of man and beast, their time has come, spirits
shall feast,
Setting sail on the Devil's tide, another voyage, oceans wide.

Heaven On Earth

In the beginning, as we know, there was Earth and Heaven,
Then rather quickly, along came the first *Homo Sapien!*
Born strong, capable and gifted,
They came, they saw and they conquered,
And over every living creature, they had dominion.

Human beings created civilisation, as they deemed fit,
Next came progress, technology and all the rest of it,
Their population grew and grew,
Ever-looking for pastures new,
Pushing the balance of nature to the very limit!

The state of the world today is not a pretty sight,
If you've not seen it lately, you're in for an awful fright!
Full exploitation, land and sea,
All of nature, taken for free!
Even our atmosphere is in such a terrible plight!

World leaders are more concerned missile sites are out of range,
Rather than the dire consequences of climate change!
Everyone is driven by greed
They take more than they really need!
And when natural resources run out, is it all so strange?

Global warming, the depletion of the ozone layer!
Uncontrolled deforestation, a man-made disaster!
Environmental pollution!
Unchecked desertification!
Extinction of endangered species, all human error!

When the children inherit this planet, what will they find?
Will there still be Heaven on Earth, what will we leave behind?
Is the land abundant and green?
Seas and skies, blue as it had been?
Will every living thing still multiply after their kind?

Faded Summers

Looking back at younger days, the endless carefree gaiety,
Was there once a charming house of passionate memory?
    I've walked that path before, more times than you can imagine,
    Breathe that familiar fragrance, a burning desire within.

See those curtains move and part, her fingers slender and neat?
Looking out the window, my lady so lovely and sweet,
    In her private fantasies, she's waiting every day,
    The one she's always longing for, a dream coming her way.

The days passed like a lifetime, nights eternally tranquil,
Sharing our deepest moments, a world where time stood still,
    Two hearts beating in tune, like it was only yesterday,
    If we were the perfect soulmates, why did love go away?

Is it really true what they say, that all good things must end?
Perhaps it's better to be a lover, to be a friend,
    We will always find cause for anger, a reason to hate,
    We only recognise true love, when it is far too late.

What becomes of shattered dreams, long after the bitter pill?
There's only emptiness, a teardrop on the window sill,
    What becomes of lonely souls, mere shadows of clouds above?
    There's always deep remorse, a circle of ill-fated love.

Have you walked that path before, faded summers of your mind?
Happy days, carefree days, leaving warm memories behind,
    Lovers join, sweet embrace, but the bliss is over too soon,
    Stars crossing in the night, two broken hearts, a sad old moon.

SHIRLEY
MACDONALD

My childhood with my four sisters, Mum, and Dad were very happy. Mum and Dad sang songs to each other as they took care of us. We always had delicious home-made food with plenty of fresh vegetables which Dad grew in our allotment.

I was born in 1942 and I do remember rationing books and gas masks hung in a cupboard.

The days seemed endless with hot summer days and lots of snow in winter. We used to fly down icy slopes on our home-made sledges that Dad had made out of tea-chests.

Everything changed when Dad died, I was ten years old. My sisters and I helped Mum and we all supported each other with love. When I was fifteen I went into dressmaking and I also babysat for a family who owned an antique shop. This is where I read poetry books which I loved.

I did not put pen to paper until later in my life, after two divorces and five children. It seemed at that time, I just felt I had to write. I was at that period taking care of people in their own homes. I just felt I had to write about my childhood and experiences of my life. I hope my poems other people will relate to and that they bring a smile or a tear to them like it does to me.

Why I write poetry is something I cannot explain, I believe there is a poet in all of us. I feel I am very lucky to be able to spread some happiness with my words.

My pen name is Shirley Cowper.

War

The word is short,
Not the actions of the word,
People's lives change
People's worlds are torn into pieces.
Why should we be destroyed?
Who wants hurt through mankind?
When we are at war, everyone is touched by it.
No one is left out.
In this world of ours, why have misery and pain?
Who wins, who loses -
Does it matter anymore?
Now we are at war, we have to live for today,
Forget those tomorrows, we might not see them.
What of our children?
Their children?
My grandchildren?
Who cares when they are at war?
I do!

To Change The World

How I wish I could change this world
Into a sea of happiness.
To take away all the pain and strife
And end all the bitterness.
To live in peace,
Peace of the mind,
Peace of the soul.
The hurting to go out of the door once more,
To live together, as we all should be
In harmony.
Heading in the right direction
To take this world and shake it up.
To make people know we have had enough.
No more suffering of any kind
Love and fulfilment through mankind.
To fill our minds with happiness,
Oh how I wish I could change this world,
Like this world should be, into a sea of happiness.

Look At Me

Take one look at me, you will see
Love bouncing out of my mind
Wanting you to catch it with open arms.
To surround me with care
You know I need you there beside me
All the time,
Memories we have to share,
Laughing eyes and searching minds.
We are one of a kind,
You know how my breathing goes when
You touch me with tender care.
Stroking faces, caressing hair,
Embraces beyond control.
Your eyes deep into my soul,
Wondering which way I would like you to go,
Nothing can ever replace our timeless love.
It is as if it has just begun.
Take a look at me and you will see.

Whitsuntide Day

We all knew our places
As we all stood in a line.
Five of us girls, how did we shine.
Hair plaited, new frocks on, new shoes on our feet.
As we all ran off, skipping down our street.
Showing off our new clothes was such a great treat.
It was Whitsuntide Sunday
We were all dressed up to the nines
As we all danced in line.
We wished it would go on forever
This Whitsuntide Day.
We never thought it would but now it has gone away.
No more new frocks on,
No more new shoes on our feet,
No more Whitsuntide Day.
Because everyone buys new shoes and clothes,
Every day of the week.

Where Have The Days Of Summer Gone?

Where have the summer days gone?
When the sun stayed out all day long.
We would play hopscotch, whipping tops, just having fun.
Sitting out with our picnics, no clouds in the sky,
Just another piece of Mum's home-made apple pie.
No rushing here, no cars on the roads,
Only one or two, the well-off owned,
That left us out.
We did not care as we loved to play out,
Hide-and-seek, kicking can, skipping ropes
Were our favourite games.
No TV to stare at when we came home,
Just our wireless that Dad had built.
We all sat around it, with delight
'Shh! Dick Barton is on!' We all listened intently
Until it finished and then we had a song.
Reading comics, sewing dresses, just having fun.
No one seems to know where those days have gone.
It seems, yesterday years,
As I sit here thinking about it,
It brings me into tears.

Sisters

When we were children, sisters of mine
You all made things worthwhile.
Four sisters I had, I was next to the youngest,
They were always there with their reassuring smiles.
Sharing you did, you spoke from your hearts,
Sensible answers gave me a start.
Those teenage years of sharing clothes, just having fun,
Another dress made, hair back-combed, high heels on,
Dancing the night away to the 'Twist',
Another Elvis song ended our night.
Homeward-bound as we were all worn out.
Sundays were special, all shops were closed,
A day of rest, it was the best.
Off to the park, dressed up to the nines
Cooling off at the coffee bar, just having fun.
Waiting for the picture house to run the latest film.
We sisters enjoyed our days,
Not like now, it's a rat-race.

Never To Part

Thoughts of you never leave my head
Whispering your name as I go to bed.
When I met you, my life went into a spin,
Just to think of you, made me dither,
No way to control it.
I just cannot believe it.
You make me feel complete
In every way, every day.
Our love I will treasure
For now and there after,
We are as one.
Our lives have just begun,
Sharing our laughter,
Sharing our sorrows,
Sharing our gladness.
Knowing we have more tomorrows,
Never to part,
Loving each other straight from our hearts.

Just You And I Will Ever Know

Today has been special
No one else will ever know,
Just you and I, as we feel our love grow.
Two hearts beating as one, as we hold on together.
Only you and I will ever know.
This love we both share and treasure.
Lips caressing each other,
Bodies entwined, going out of our minds.
Only you and I will ever know,
Eyes for each other, senses have lost control
Emotions of love surrounds us,
No boundaries will stop us,
We have our love for each other
That is all we two need to know.

Whitby By The Sea

Oh! What a place to be,
Walking around Whitby,
The seagulls soaring above the clouds
As the crowds wandering around
The sun, having fun.
Oh what a place to be near the sea.
Watching the boats coming into moor.
Exciting faces as they show off their catch.
The smell of fish and chips and all that
Cannot be matched.
As people sit down looking out to the sea
Dreaming of faraway places
Where they would like to be.
Who would want to swop Whitby? Not me!

My Grandchildren

I had one, now I have many
How they make me feel complete.
Just to hear their laughter
Stays with me today and after.
Each one has their problems, come what may.
We sit together, watching their favourite video
Being safe.
In this world, who knows what's around the corner?
As long as Grandma is there to share their laughter.
Dressing up, painting faces, flying kites, riding bikes,
Singsongs, baking cakes, just having fun.
Bath time is crazy.
Grandma blowing bubbles over them in the bath as
Their water guns, they give them a blast.
Bedtime is here, another storybook is read
As they slip into bed.
Voices shout out as I turn down the light,
'Goodnight Grandma for being our best friend.'
Tears in my eyes as I kiss them goodnight.
Just to hear them all happy, is music to my ears.
I am going to be around them all
For lots and lots of years.

My Daughter

Busy mum is what she is
Fitting in her busy day,
List for this and list for that,
One more problem must be solved.
How she keeps her sanity, one will never know.
Rushing here to bring things back,
No time to smell the flowers, no time at all.
She recalls her happiest hours
When she was single, living in her flat.
Nothing to think about, only buying a new hat.
What hat to wear? What dress to put on?
Now I'm afraid that has all gone.
To be a mum is what we crave for
Taking care of babies.
We do not realise,
Right before our eyes,
How life is slipping away
As you start another busy day.

To Walk By The Sea

What a wonderful day for me,
As I prepare to go off to see the sea.
How I have missed those walks by the sea,
Feeling the waves caress my feet.
The air is clean,
The breeze touches my cheek
As I walk on the beach.
The seagulls cry out as they swoop down to me,
The sun appears to greet us, mirroring faces
On the sea.
What a wonderful place to be near the sea,
Nothing can replace this moment.
As I stroll on and on with the sun,
Sea and sand around me.
Picking up the shells as I go along,
Feeling nothing but contentment.
To be able to see and touch life's untold precious
Gifts, forever with me
To walk by the sea.

My Grandson Who Lives Far Away

I have a grandson who lives far away,
How I miss him, words cannot say,
All I have are photographs on my wall.
His large brown eyes looking at me
As I walk past him in the hall.
How do I miss him, my bundle of joy,
Soon he will be walking and talking and
I won't be there,
Soon he will be a big boy.
Things I miss about my grandson, no one seems to care,
I just want to hold him, this grandson of mine,
To pick him up and let him know I am around.
I am that lady who sends him some fun,
Plenty of books, letters and unusual toys.
Wish I was there when the postman arrives,
Things could have been different
If you didn't live far away,
We could have played together, day after day.
I could have read those stories,
I could have kissed you goodnight.
It is not to be.
The miles will never stop me loving you from afar,
You are my grandson wherever you are.
Another letter posted,
Another book on its way.
To my favourite grandson
Who lives very far away.

Love Grandma

DEREK PLUCK

Was born on the 5th March 1951. He was educated at Merrywood Grammar School, Bristol and the University of London, where he was awarded Bachelor of Science and Doctor of Philosophy degrees and a post-graduate teaching certificate.

For the last twenty-nine years Derek has resided in Preston, Lancashire. Until he took early retirement, in July 2006, Derek was a lecturer in Biological and Environmental Sciences to students of Preston College and the University of Central Lancashire.

Derek has been writing poetry since he was seventeen as a means of recording his impressions and feelings and of interpreting these and communicating them to others. He regards Edward Thomas, Ted Walker and Alexandros Baras as the main influences on his poetic themes and styles. He seeks to combine the precise observations of a naturalist and scientist with the skills of a landscape painter, taking images from the 'camera of the mind', shaping them and interpreting them on the canvas of the page.

Dr Pluck is passionate about heritage and natural history; he has a poignant sense of time and place and an eye for detail. He frequently uses mystical or sexual imagery and reflects on wildlife and landscapes with a combination of air, earth, light, fire and water.

In addition to English Heritage, natural history and conservation, Derek enjoys keeping tropical aquarium fish, touring Britain and Europe and collecting strange friends. During his retirement he plans to do more creative writing and is currently working on his first novel.

He has a twenty-five year old daughter, Rachel, a graduate in Sports Science from the University of Central Lancashire and he now lives with his second wife, Christine. He has two stepdaughters: Juliet and Melanie and two grandchildren, by marriage, Danielle and Bianca.

Derek has been published in nine previous 'Spotlight Poets' publications and has almost two hundred poems published in other anthologies and poetry magazines.

A Toast

Scarlet goblets, splashed bright
With the wine of recent rain
And a conspiracy of early light;
The wet red, rather than a dry white,
Apparently for no other reason
Than a celebration of the season,
These large tulips raised high,
As if offering up a toast to May;
Perhaps we too should lift our cups,
Which, for once, runneth over, so
Here's to us my love, bottoms up.

Flamingos

In their habits, preferring to be gregarious;
In display, certainly comical, if not hilarious;
Their colour and movement an extravaganza
On the magic landscapes of the memory;
Salmon-pink, though not through eating fish;
Necks curved, heads below the water-line
Beaks, like sieves, straining pink crustacea
And algae to give pigment to their plumage;
Seeming aloof, almost haughty in posture
But dance-like as they move, tall in stature;
All long legs, folded wings as feathered skirts,
A naughty glimpse of their pink frilly panties
And an ankle seeming where a knee might be;
What a performance, strutting-their-stuff:
A flamenco by flamingos, evolving to a tango
As they boogie to a music that is visual but,
For the record and artistic impression's sake,
We reflect upon the intricate routine, as the
Original choreography is mirrored by the lake.

Thoughts Of Robin
(In memory of my friend Robin Day)

Solemn words at this most poignant
Time, the sad, yet fond, moments
Of this farewell, as Robin's ashes mingle
With the earth in this churchyard; the tingle
As the hairs stand up on the back of my neck.
Yet I still remember Robin, large as life,
At the theatre with us and Val, his wife;
We had many things in common, we talked
Of poetry, cameras and experiences of
Travel and our shared enjoyment of the
Herefordshire we knew, around Ledbury
Where he grew up, in a magic landscape
Of cider-apple orchards and mistletoe.
It is these memories, I'm pleased to find,
Keep Robin very much alive, inside my mind;
Hopes of a new beginning, not just the end,
For a man I respected, found interesting
And was proud to think of as my friend.

Impressions Of A Landscape
(Burton Agnes Hall)

Light coming through the windows
Of this Tudor red-brick masterpiece,
Highlights bright colours in these works
Of well known French Impressionists
Upon the walls - leaving images blurred
And the artists' hues seemingly slurred
Upon the canvas, making one step
Back a pace, before the detail is revealed;
Each picture neatly framed and arranged
With care upon the walls of this gallery
While I look out the window, staring
Into the face of early summer, in her
Shy smile of this late May afternoon -
Before she averts her blue-green eyes
To where I see truly golden oilseed rape
Splashed warm upon this landscape,
In pigments mixed on palette of the sun
And daubed wildly on this outdoor canvas;
While wind caresses the green fields
Of wheat, framed rough with hedgerows,
Preferring such paintings, as a rule,
From this contemporary English school,
Where daylight, colour and texture hybridise
To sketch an image of the Yorkshire Wolds,
Making a lasting impression on my eyes.

Catkins

(Quite lucky after all)

Showering a gold upon the grey,
Chandeliers of catkins light the way -
Reflecting the cold watery sunlight
Back into my only half-awaken eyes,
Illuminating this damp February day;
While I dwell on what is and might be,
Winter, it seems, springs a surprise -
Making this day unseasonally bright,
Replacing my feelings of resentment
With an inner calm's contentment;
My thoughts transfigured and for me
It seems that finally, I see the light.

Prague

(For Christine)

From the castle, looking down below -
Where the wide Vltava river flows
Beneath the many ancient arches
Of Charles Bridge, through this city's
Golden dream; while in the distance
A proliferation of church towers,
Coloured domes and shapely spires,
Like a Central European Oxford,
Painted bright upon the inner eye
And all along the historic waterside:
Baroque, Renaissance and Gothic;
Almost the same scene that inspired
Both Smetana and Dvorak and fired
Their imaginations to evoke in music
A timeless depth of feeling, romantic
Spirit and a sense of national pride.

Rose Of Sharon

Among the foliage, there are much brighter
And, clearly, much more ostentatious flowers
In the garden, but how quick their gaudy
Petals seem to fade and fall - while my eyes
Instead, are drawn to more subtle beauty;
Your seductive smile reflects like sunlight,
Warming not the skin, but the heart within;
Or as stars, twinkling in a summer twilight,
Under a green-leafed canopy of coming night;
The shrub, a whole star-studded galaxy
Whose constellations I've grown to understand;
Tending the bush with a gardener's loving care,
An experience of nature's Heaven in my hand.

Berkeley Castle

(Rose-red city, half as old as time)

A pale, late August, sun softly washes
The stout walls of this ancient citadel,
So that the warmth on stone blushes
A deeper shade of pink along the curves
And battlements of a sumptuous castle
That I have come to know so well.
Yet secrets held within this fortress
Keep - might echo tales of an evil thing,
Of Hell's dark deed, in the murder of a king;
But for us today, such thoughts have gone;
The rounded beauty of the ornamental shell
Rising, as a dream of some lost Avalon,
From the placid, lake-like surface
Of damp green fields; a rose-red snail
Crawling over a dew-soaked grass -
As I look out towards the wild saltmarsh
Strands, fringing a sleepy River Severn,
Across Berkeley's rich and verdant vale.

Fuchsias

From the leafy belfries
Of foliage, in a red-veined
Green, stamen-clappers,
Long and hanging-down
Inside the swollen bells
Of these Fuchsia flowers,
Ringing-out in season's
Colours; a celebration
In bright pink and crimson
And echoes, loud in
Purple and vermilion;
Swinging up and down
Until their sweet sound
Is interpreted by the eye;
Tolling in close harmony,
As late summer's melody
Stays in tune, driven by
The rhythm of the wind.

Three Cliffs Bay

(The Gower Peninsula)

At a distance, a dead dinosaur of rocks,
With a Stegosaurus profile of spines
Upon its back - its carcass on the sand,
Looking beyond - the lazy, serpentine
River meanders, in a blue of Heaven,
Across a beach brought here from paradise,
Towards its destiny in white surge of tide:
In stark contrast to this tropical island dream,
The rugged scenery, perhaps a touch alpine
In character, with sharper peaks of stone,
Looking like a cliff top view of *Toblerone*
And, in the foreground, beauty personified,
However incongruous this might seem,
By a Lulworth Cove of sleepy blue lagoon
Encircled; bathing in the growing wonder
Of sun-struck gold of a summer afternoon.

Sunset At Worms Head

Rocky silhouette of this Welsh dragon,
Woken from the depths of slumber,
By the surging slurp of tide in flood;
Tail severed from the mainland -
Roaring defiance in a fiery breath,
Causing dark clouds to smoulder
At their edges in the western sky
And deeper violet shades of twilight,
To ignite in gold and crimson flame
And silver sea to redden with its blood.

Wind Turbines
(Cornwall)

On the windswept cliff tops,
These strange rotating giants,
Harvesting the power of the wind,
Seem in sympathy with landscape -
Adding a new dimension
To the stunning scenery;
Bright white propellers turning
Like a squadron, scrambled
Ready for take-off - towards
A brave and greener future.

Meerkats

In a row, standing erect and alert, your
Paler bellies visible and both forepaws
Held together on your lower abdomens;
A contrasting strip of stripes on your backs,
Like a defensive wall of footballers,
Intent on protecting their groins, just prior to
The taking of a free kick. Those sharp claws,
For digging, clearly visible - while sentries
Keep watch and the rest just sunbathe,
Snouts sawn-off and mouths curved in grins
Beneath and behind black button-noses
And lighter colour fur of your receding chins;
Eyes focussed on the distance of horizon
As if pushed up against a single telescope.

Mistletoe

(Herefordshire)

Startled, the colony of rooks
Explodes from still-leafless oaks,
Upon the tapestry of silence,
In a shrapnel of deep purple -
Leaving just goitres of mistletoe,
Like a malignancy that chokes
These large and ancient trees,
Bleeding much of their life away,
Depriving them of the minerals
From the rich and fertile soils
Deep in the heart of England.
Yet also, rooted in our pagan
Superstitions, it is incongruous
And, after all, poetic justice
That we harvest this parasite,
White-berried and in its prime,
For one of our Christian festivals -
Along with the holly and the ivy -
Nature's celebration of fertility,
Stealing a kiss at Christmas time,
And even stranger, as a source
Of drugs for cancer chemotherapy.

Angela With Giraffes

It's enough to make you want to laugh,
The very idea of stroking a giraffe;
I'd have considered it inconceivable,
Yet here is my dear friend, Angela
Patting the brown-cream, maculated
Neck of this five-metre camelopard;
Face-to-face on this aerial walkway,
The experience is almost unbelievable:
Aware of its long black eyelashes,
Tiny, tubular ears - a touch comical -
A bumpy forehead and large knobbly
Horns; its grey-blue tongue reaches
Out and curls around the willow leaves
She holds out to feed the creature;
A miracle of harmony with this giraffe,
The composition of my photograph
Is perfect, the two complement each
Other: slender, elegant and beautiful,
Captured also by the camera of the
Memory, a view both rare and wonderful.

JEANNE SAGAR

'Consciousness comes from knowing where you are from, what forces have formed you and what are acting upon you. You enter history when you shape the things that are happening to your advantage, otherwise you are just swept along'.

(A quotation from an article by the late Fred Hollows - Eye Surgeon and a great humanitarian - 1993)

This is one of my favourite quotations. It reminds me of how I feel about writing my own poetry and reading the poems of others. Poetry enables me to explore within myself, my world - who I am in relation to others - where I have come from - what I am doing now and where maybe I am going. To reassess and re-evaluate and hopefully give pleasure to others whilst taking them into my world, if only for a few moments.

2am

Silver shafts and shapes of moonlight
Kaleidoscope into the room
All is still and luminous
A silvery wonderland
Time seems suspended
Encapsulated and cocooned
Life's circadian rhythms pulsing gently
And through the open window
Come pungent odours
The Earth is breathing
Soon the dawn will break
And La Luna's radiant beams
Ethereal splendour and cosmic power
Will shine and serve elsewhere
Until we come full circle
And turn to greet her radiant
Shimmering delights once more

Summer '70

I lost myself that summer
Along the cliffs and sandy bays of Pembrokeshire
Wandering along the shore
Wherever constant is the sea
I left a part of me
Among the rocks and pools
And pebbles smooth
I'd like to walk there once again
Where stars shine down
And cast their sparkle on the waves
Where sand, surf, wind and sun
And the music, oh yes the music
All came together
For one brief, exhilarating
Shining moment

Bus Stop

Hail, rain, snow or shine, there she'd be waiting for the bus
Perennial cheap raincoat belted tightly
Around her wasted body
Wispy hair and pinched pale face
Spots of crimson rouge rubbed into hollow cheeks
Bright coral lipstick upon her lips
Bare spindly legs, fire-scorched and mottled
Tottering in white high heels
Always she stood apart; perpetually marooned it seemed
Inside an untouchable space
And as she climbed on-board, passengers
Surreptitiously leaned away, for fear she might touch them
There would be whispers, nudges, furtive glances
A palpable discomfort: no one ever spoke to her
And yet she held her ground and person bravely
With a quiet, haughty, almost desperate bravado
Her way of coping and facing the world I guess
She was a woman who was different
Did someone love her? - I hope so
And now and then I think of her
This fragile woman
Dressed in raincoat, high heels, handbag and glass beads
Quietly waiting for a bus to take her to town

Sailing Away

Oh, the big ship sails on the Illy, Illy, O
Early in the morning

We sailed away on a cruising ship to a tropical paradise
Watched the far horizon moving up and down
Endless food, non-stop entertainment
Serviced and cosseted all the way
We paraded the deck and explored the ship
Three days sailing to beautiful islands
To find a tropical palette of rising green
Floating in a glistening sea
We crowded on deck to see colourful islanders
Singing and dancing, hustling, bustling
Smiling faces; luminous eyes, dark and wistful
Amazing unbelievable heat, excitement, exotica
Intoxicating perfumes and balmy air

I'd dreamed of these islands
Of sapphire-blue seas, endless skies
And palm-fringed beaches
Sparkling white sand; tiny boats hugging the shore

Smiling Shem took us to town
His taxi - his pride and joy
Lovingly preserved with tape and string
I was glad to spend my dollars here
We drove through town to see bustling markets
Old stately buildings, faded legacies of colonisation
Past silent, long-limbed young men
Watching us, watching them, indifferently
Laughing children playing, running
Groups of islanders gathering food
Women with babies keeping busy
Clusters of men sitting silently
Under fragile huts of poles and palm leaves
A resilient people with very little

It started to rain, heavy tropical stuff
Drenching everything and everyone
Sun and sparkle stripped away
But just as quickly as it came, the deluge stopped
The sun came out and all was as before - transformed

Then eventually, our time was up, so we turned around
And headed back to our floating home upon the sea
To coolness and comfort; dinner awaits
And yet, for all our luxury, cosseting and care
I knew we'd lost something very special
Qualities that these smiling people still possess
A unique richness in life, while living simply
On their beautiful islands across the seas

Oh, the big ship sails on the Illy, Illy, O
Early in the morning

Enigma

You are my dead - you cannot speak
And to my sorrow your numbers grow
And with everlasting regret
I let you slip away like sand
Falling through my fingers
Taking with you secrets, codes and information
Vital missing pieces of the jigsaw of life
Leaving worrying, disappointing spaces
Where the 'Bluebird of Happiness' should be
Stuff that would have made me whole, a star
If this were Hollywood
I could bring you back to life with my tears
Or perhaps a kiss
I'd animate you into being - oh how I wish?
But here I am, living life's movie
Bobbin' along at the O.K. Corral
The cameras keep rolling and the credits scrolling
The players are assembled, the director's ready
My make-up's in place and the show must go on
Quiet please and *action!*

La Mer Goes Digital

I saw my heart yesterday - courtesy of ultrasound
Saw what makes me live and breathe: I watched the screen and
Was reminded of the sea - my heart's surface divided into quadrants
Being scanned just as the beam of a lighthouse sweeps the sea
Searching for features - pin-pointing hazards
I heard a sonar beep echoing, sound waves bouncing back
My heart's rhythm, sucking, squelching
I saw a tiny demented, stick-like arm waving jerkily
A crooked finger beckoning constantly, back and forth
Opening and closing incessantly - a heart valve
Then a cut-away tube appeared
With curves and peaks rolling along its length
Like waves in the ocean - highs and lows pushing on relentlessly
Next, an orgy and explosion of volatile colours
Pulsing and swirling, primeval gases in a mini-universe
Electric blues, greens, yellows and red
We were voyeurs, the technician and I
Viewing a masterpiece of nature
Like two sub-mariners of the deep, on a mission to explore my heart
How does it keep on beating, continually renewing itself?
I thought of the technology that allows this exploration
And then of the greater gift given by two people
Each with their own imprint
Who created me
And the amazingness of what I feel
Leaves me breathless

Beautiful People

I see them, the young
Their amazing beauty
Soft dewy freshness, firm glowing skin
Shining eyes, agile minds
Lustrous hair and strong bones
Running, jumping, energy unlimited
Supple bodies ever moving, untouched by time

Old age they say, is the most
Surprising thing that happens to us
That we are shocked and amazed
To one day find that we are old

When I was very young
People beyond twenty-five seemed ancient
Ah, the sweet ignorance of youth
Age, I now know is relative
Depending where on the time scale we are
In my thirties, forty sounded tragic
At forty, I felt fifty would be old
Yet reaching fifty didn't feel so bad
Because arriving at sixty would be devastating

Growing closer to one's biblical
Three-score-years and ten gives food for thought
Now, maybe reaching eighty will be perfectly acceptable
And ninety, well that's getting old
And over one hundred, yes well . . .

As I get older, I'm manipulating the bench-marks
Reassessing my views
Playing psychological and emotional mind-games with myself
Justifying, adjusting
Working out the pluses and the minuses
And when it's all too worrisome -
Trying not to think at all
Hoping it might go away

But then I think of the elders I have known
Bodies grown frail - gradual loss - a fraying of edges
And I remember that they too
Once had their time in the sun
Glowing and radiant, dancing and singing
Moving gracefully - bodies at ease
Looking to the future
The beautiful people, beautiful memories
Moments in time
I close my eyes and I see them
And I am at peace

Silver Scissors

Six days a week he rides into town
To ply his trade
Keen of eye and deft of hand
The man with the silver scissors
His clients are waiting
First he observes; then skilfully lifts strands of hair
Running fingers this way and that
Determining the move and flow
Feel and texture, lift and fall
Not really for him the wash and dry
Colour and curl; the cut is all
He studies each angle, analysing face and form
Searching for proportion, style and balance
Reflected in the polished glass
Weighing up the pros and cons
Then with comb and scissors poised, he starts
Cutting, snipping, smoothing, combing
Paring back the layers, creating perfect symmetry
With flair, talent and consummate skills
Practised and perfected throughout the years
This is the man with the silver scissors
Oh may he never leave town

Brown Paper Parcels

'Oh no, here we go - we need new clothes'
So off we'd be taken
To the tall terraced house of Sarah the buxom
Sarah with the gingery hair, Marcel waves and wrap-around-plaits
Golden coins fell from her ears - golden rings upon her fingers
Sarah was different, she was a diddykie, a travelling person
Then down into Sarah's front room we'd troop
And there stacked along walls and floor, were row upon row
Of brown paper parcels of every shape and size, tied up with string
Sarah dealt in second-hand stuff, bought from the better-off people
Good clothes with labels, worn for a while, then discreetly sold on
'It's all good stuff isn't it?' my mother and Sarah kept saying
Their eagle eyes missing nothing
But first - the criteria
Would it last, did it have big hems, and would it wash?
Colour didn't matter, nor the texture or style
You got what you got: and when we'd finished trying on
And our new clothes were parcelled up
Sarah made a pot of tea; there'd be a chat and a reckoning-up
On a scrap of paper with indelible pencil
And we'd depart with 'it's all good stuff' ringing in our ears
Of course it was because it was made for the better-off people
People with different needs - people who lived in a different world
And that's how Sarah, with her recycled good stuff
Sarah of the travelling people (entrepreneur extraordinaire)
Made a living, whilst filling a gap and clothing the poor

Dreaming

Fly me home silver bird to my place of birth
The land of seasons
Deliver me to my secret places
To gaze into dappled waters
Where golden kingcups, the marshy marigolds
Hold their court
Let me touch fern and moss and ancient stone
Sit beneath the glorious trees and smell the new-mown hay
Scan the lonely hills and valleys
Wander through hamlet, village and town
Walk in the footsteps of my people
Remembering those who went before

Then bring me back silver bird
To a sun-baked land, where fire is supreme
And where grow the tall, tall trees
Fauna and flora exotic and spectacular
Amazing wildlife, captivating and dangerous
Undiscovered unbelievable places
Enticing the adventurous
To a vast and empty hinterland
With a burning red heart
Where an ancient people live their dreamtime
And a new people have brought their dreams

Then eventually, silver bird
Fly me to my 'special' home
Far away at the ends of the Earth
To Aotearoa
Fly me over azure-jewelled islands
From north to south
To gaze upon the snow-capped sentinels
Ngauruhoe, Ruapehu, Taranaki, Aorangi
Then finally, set me down on Papatuanuku
Where I feel safe
And when the night-time comes

Cover me with Ranginui's velvet cloak of darkest blue
Sprinkled with a million stars
Then I will stand on sunny wind-swept beaches
And scan the far horizons
Breathing in the purest air
This is the home of the Tangatawhenua
The people of the land
That holds and shelters my loved ones

So where is my real home silver bird?
For each of these places have claimed a part of me
But inevitably, I will go to Aotearoa
To the Land of the Long White Cloud
For there is the future, the present and past
This is the one that calls me the most

But remember silver bird
There's still one last amazing flight
The most adventurous of all
When you will take me to my final home
And when we've received the relevant clearance
For us to ascend higher than we've ever been before
When boarding is complete - the runway clear
And permission for take-off is granted
Then, silver bird, you can fly me home
To my last great, ultimate destination

BERYL THORNBURY

Born on Merseyside and educated at Bootle Grammar School for Girls, Beryl has, since her school days, been a keen singer, and became a well-known soprano in clubs and theatreland throughout the north-west, Wales and the Isle of Man.

She developed her style of writing through her association with the diverse characters and characteristics of stage folk, invariably based on the friendship and fun of her colleagues.

Her many talents include script writing, acting, sketching and painting. These are in addition to her domestic skills of cooking the joint, baking the bread, and brewing the proverbial 'cuppa' without which her flair for light-hearted dialogue may be deflected.

Beryl has broadcast on BBC and has appeared on TV in Coronation Street, Emmerdale, Boon, Medics and many dramas. She provides a little light relief with her humour during those long spells of inactivity during rehearsals.

Beryl has already established a reputation among her friends for the fun she introduces into her work. Her parodies of musicals and plays produced by local theatre groups and amateur operatic societies, give scope to her recognition of the understanding of wit and wisdom.

In Liverpool she was employed in the post office drawing office where she met her husband Bill. They now live in Stockport, have three sons and a home in Malta.

Enlivened by a wealth of gathered anecdotes, there is plenty more verse in the think tank.

The Truth About Teeth

A visit to the dentist
Is a trip to the unknown,
And while waiting for your turn to come,
You may just hear a groan.

At first you're lured into the chair
And asked to, 'Open wide'
Then after careful scrutiny
The dentist may confide

'I'll give you an injection,
You will like it, it's pain killing'
In fact though, in reality,
It's much worse than the drilling.

In next to no time you will find
Your nose has gone to sleep
Which is just as well having been informed
'This eye tooth goes very deep'

'Quite deep,' he says again, with glee
His eyes now getting meaner,
As he hangs upon your bottom jaw
A mini vacuum cleaner.

He says, 'It sucks out all the debris,
And the water and the blood,
Come now, don't be cowardly,
It's really very good.'

'Now aim the rinse at the basin please,'
He says with anxious glare,
But at last the job is finished and
You can climb out of the chair.

'In six months time I'll see you then,'
Comes the call as you head for the door.
But chronic deafness now sets in,
And the comment you choose to ignore.

Enough's enough you now decide,
The mem'ry will take time to fade,
And you'll never admit that the fault is all yours,
And the truth is you're just plain afraid.

To The Future

Folk often talk of the *'good old days'*,
When recalling times gone by,
Reliving happy memories,
Some accompanied by a sigh.

And it's good to reminisce
And bring history to mind,
But let's not forget the present,
For it's passed us by we'll find.

These days are so important
We are in the here and now,
Shaping our own futures,
'Thou we don't know where or how.

We must greet each day with pleasure,
As tomorrow's still brand new.
These are the *'good old days'* of the future,
So sit back, enjoy the view.

If We Can Help

We missed the morning sickness,
And the heartburn and the cramp,
And thinking of new babies
Makes our eyes go kind of damp.
We didn't share the backache,
Or the swollen legs and feet,
But we're waiting quite impatiently
The little one to meet.
We won't be there at midnight
When she's asking to be fed,
We'll likely have our feet up,
And a drink in hand instead.
But if there's something we can do
Then please don't fail to ask,
Cos pulling funny faces,
Even cooing proves no task.
For after all it's not our style
Or our intent to shirk,
It's just *not fair* to sit back
And let you do all the work.

Doom And Gloom

Menu

Doom and gloom on toast	*Off*
Madness au gratin	£2.50
Depression grilled or fried	£3.50
Phobia casserolled	£2.99
Anxiety hot or cold	£1.85
Worry devilled	£4.50
Kindness organic	*No charge*

The doom and gloom is off today,
The menu's incomplete,
But if you'd like some madness
Then you'll find it quite a treat.
Depression isn't going well,
It's just that time of year,
Yet phobia's a winner,
We can meet 'most any fear.
Anxiety, now there's a thing,
It takes on many a twist,
A luxury most folk confess
They really can't resist.
You may prefer a worry,
Or you could have three or four,
There's certainly no shortage,
We don't need them, *that's* for sure.
Perhaps a cup of kindness
Would be nearer to your taste,
If so, sit back, enjoy it,
It's not good to drink in haste.
We hope you'll recommend us
For our service is unique,
Please call again if you should find
You're feeling faint and weak.

So What!

Have you ever noticed after tossing half the night
To make the pillow comfy and the duvet fit just right
No sooner have you fixed it, and are floating on a cloud,
It's then the birds begin to sing and the alarm rings good and loud?

Or when you're washing dishes and the sink is full of suds,
The postman rings the doorbell, 'Will you sign please for the goods?'
It wouldn't seem to matter if the parcels were for you,
But they're always for the neighbours, so you have to sign in lieu.

Then often on a Sunday when the roast is done a treat,
And you've rounded up the family with cries of, 'Come and eat,'
The telephone decides to ring, it's Auntie Flo again,
Or telesales for windows which they swear will stop the rain.

The moral of this story is don't lie awake at night
Awaiting the dawn chorus as the sky is getting light.
And never mind the dishes or the soapsuds in the sink,
If the postman rings the doorbell say, 'Come in and have a drink.'

And as for Auntie Florrie and that double glazing chap,
Invite them round together then go off and have a nap.
It doesn't matter what you do as long as you enjoy it,
And whatever use philosophy if no one will employ it?

Yesterday has gone for good, tomorrow? Yet unknown,
But if we try we might just find our destiny's our own.
We should aim to seek some pleasure in the daily trials and tasks,
And say we find life wonderful - if anybody asks.

The Takeover

An addition to the family
Is exciting, there's no doubt,
But there's much to learn and master,
That's what life is all about.
A baby needs attention,
And will feed from morn till night,
But when smiles replace the crying
Then you'll know you've got it right.
A puppy is a pleasure,
But may send you round the bend,
Then suddenly you notice
He's turned into man's best friend.
Not so the artificial brain,
Complete with screen and mouse
It will take you over day and night,
Once you let it in your house.
You'll feel confused and stupid
When it won't obey your rules,
And if there's someone watching
You're the biggest of all fools.
But don't give up, you're winning,
Just be careful of the traps,
Be firm with it from time to time,
Or raise your voice, perhaps.
Yes!
Working the computer
Is a dangerous task, it's true,
For almost before you know it
The computer's working you.

Stay In Touch

I've used the high street bank now
For a good few years and more,
Paid bills by direct debit
And had cheque books by the score.
I've got a roll of statements
Fit to paper any room,
All neatly filed in order,
Lest I need them I presume.
The automated cashpoint,
I've become quite used to that,
'Tho I find it rather lacking
If I'm feeling like a chat.
But now I've found the phone bank,
It's the ultimate indeed,
Transactions are quite painless
And it fills my every need.
The tellers are so friendly
As they talk me through each deal,
But when checked out for security
What an idiot I feel.
That special name, important date,
They just won't come to mind,
Likewise my favourite colour,
I've forgotten it I find.
I do thank them for their patience,
It's appreciated much,
And to prove it in the future
I will surely *stay in touch*.

Curtain Up

Think of *fifty* as the interval
Between acts one and two
Time to recharge your batteries
And do what you have to do.
You've come to know the characters
Who made up every scene,
Sometimes reading between the lines
To guess what might have been.
The story never once stood still,
No, it twisted and it turned,
And come the second act it's time
To enjoy all those things you've learned.
For this play is not a tragedy,
No matter what you've heard,
It's a scintillating thriller
In the true sense of the word.
So here's to the second *fifty*,
Raise the curtain on act two,
May *health* and *happiness* be yours,
With *laugh lines* right on cue.

Suzanne's Logic

Life is different these days,
With computers and such things,
And we know that time speeds by so fast
It surely must have wings.
Now when counting up our birthdays
Sixty's really forty-two,
At least that's what Sue told us,
So what are we to do?
When questioned on the subject
She just smiled a knowing grin,
And came up with this little verse
With which her case to win.
'What about the weekends?
You can't count those, you know,
I only age on weekdays,
So they will have to go.
Then there's Christmas, New Year, Easter,
Exempt and wrinkle-free,
And during the hours of darkness
Time stands still above the knee
So
Let's add up those weekends
The bank holidays and such,
And the long dark nights of winter
When the ageing just can't touch.
And we'll come up with the reason
For Suzanne's eternal youth,
But we'll be adding on the Saints' Days
Just in case she's telling the truth.

Computing For Idiots

To be sure you're sitting comfortably
Is important in many ways,
For it's likely you'll forget the time,
And be there for several days.
First lift the lid, I've mastered that,
Then switch the power on,
Go through the warm up process,
But where's that arrow gone?
'It's called a mouse,' said the teacher,
Showing patience beyond his years,
But I'm not too keen on vermin,
And this stirred up endless fears.
All calm again, we carry on,
Instructions flowing fast,
I lie in wait to catch the beast
As it comes running past.
I've caught it, now I'm doing well,
I'll click on here and there
And see what happens on the screen,
Oh dear, it's just a blurr.
So it goes through day and night,
By now I'm getting better,
Autumn turns to winter,
And I've written half a letter.
Tutor Paul is wilting now,
He nibbles at his pen,
As he realises I don't yet know
How to close it down again.

Drunk? Certainly Not

Drinking wine a lot'll make you drunk,
But drink it by the bottle and you're sunk,
The object of abuse and ridicule,
They'll make out you're no use and just a fool.
But once you've done your training you're OK.
You'll master certain skills along the way,
Then drink it by the flagon if you wish,
And pretend you're on the wagon, soberish.
The secret lies in making *others* think
Their judgement's somewhat dodgy - on the blink.
Try looking just off centre when you chat,
They'll end up feeling queasy - just like that.
Or looking straight but saying not a word,
They'll wonder what they've missed and should have heard.
And so you're off the hook, your battle's won,
You've proved your point and had your bit of fun.
At last the time has come - it's off to bed
To sleep off that dull throbbing in your head - sh! Sh! *Sh!*

This poem carries a health warning
Don't try it.

spotlight poets

For Better Or Worse, In Sickness Or In Health

Our local general hospital
Is not what is used to be,
Though seeming large in days gone by
There were signs for all to see.
There was 'Outpatients' and 'X-ray'
And the 'Fracture Clinic' too,
And wards just off the corridor,
I recall there were quite a few.
All this was set in spacious grounds
With hardly a car in sight,
Yet parking places were everywhere,
No need to queue or fight.
But recently the powers that be
Decided on a change,
'We'll build until there's no land left,
Who cares if the place looks strange?'
And this has surely come to pass,
New clinics now abound,
With 'X-ray 1' and 'X-ray 2'
There's confusion all around.
Two 'Out Patients' have now followed suit,
Way down the other way.
Improvement is what they call it,
Well, what more can I say?

Information

We hope you have enjoyed reading this book - and that you will continue to enjoy it in the coming years.

If you are interested in becoming a Spotlight Poet then drop us a line, or give us a call, and we'll send you a free information pack.

Alternatively, if you would like to order further copies of this book or any of our other titles, then please give us a call or log onto our website at www.forwardpress.co.uk.

Spotlight Poets Information
Remus House
Coltsfoot Drive
Peterborough
PE2 9JX
(01733) 898101